For my family, especially my mom and dad, who believe in and inspire me.

7-99

Windows Vista®: Home Networking

Joli Ballew

PUBLISHED BY
Microsoft Press
A Division of Microsoft Corporation
One Microsoft Way
Redmond, Washington 98052-6399

Library of Congress Control Number: 2007934736

Printed and bound in the United States of America.

1 2 3 4 5 6 7 8 9 QWT 2 1 0 9 8 7

Distributed in Canada by H.B. Fenn and Company Ltd.

A CIP catalogue record for this book is available from the British Library.

Microsoft Press books are available through booksellers and distributors worldwide. For further information about international editions, contact your local Microsoft Corporation office or contact Microsoft Press International directly at fax (425) 936-7329. Visit our Web site at www.microsoft.com/mspress. Send comments to mspinput@microsoft.com.

Microsoft, Active Directory, ActiveX, Internet Explorer, MSDN, OneCare, Windows, Windows Live, Windows Media, Windows Mobile, Windows Server, Windows Vista, Xbox, and Xbox 360 are either registered trademarks or trademarks of Microsoft Corporation in the United States and/or other countries. Other product and company names mentioned herein may be the trademarks of their respective owners.

The example companies, organizations, products, domain names, e-mail addresses, logos, people, places, and events depicted herein are fictitious. No association with any real company, organization, product, domain name, e-mail address, logo, person, place, or event is intended or should be inferred.

This book expresses the author's views and opinions. The information contained in this book is provided without any express, statutory, or implied warranties. Neither the authors, Microsoft Corporation, nor its resellers, or distributors will be held liable for any damages caused or alleged to be caused either directly or indirectly by this book.

Acquisitions Editor: Juliana Aldous Atkinson
Developmental Editor: Sandra Haynes
Project Editor: Melissa von Tschudi-Sutton
Editorial Production: Happenstance Type-O-Rama
Cover design: Tom Draper Design

Body Part No. X14-06306

CONTENTS

Introduction   xi

Part I Getting Started   1

Chapter 1   Introduction to Networking   3
What Windows Vista Offers   4
Why You Need a Network   4
Types of Network Configurations   5
Types of Network Hardware   8
Additional Network Terms to Know   13
Chapter Summary   15

Chapter 2   Get Ready!   17
Configure Your Windows Vista–Based PC   18
Configure Windows Firewall   24
Configure Windows Defender   26
Chapter Summary   30

Part II Setting Up a Network   31

Chapter 3   The Direct Connection Network   33
Create Workgroup Names   34
Physically Connect the Two PCs   35
Turn On Network Discovery on the Windows Vista–Based PC   36
Share the Host's Internet Connection   38
Add a Second Windows Vista–Based PC   39
Add a Windows XP–Based PC   39
Get Help for Networking Older PCs   43
Chapter Summary   44

What do you think of this book? We want to hear from you!

Microsoft is interested in hearing your feedback so we can continually improve our books and learning resources for you. To participate in a brief online survey, please visit:

www.microsoft.com/learning/booksurvey/

Chapter 4	**The Wired Ethernet Network**	**45**
	Connect the Hardware	46
	Personalize Your Network	50
	Add PCs	55
	Chapter Summary	62
Chapter 5	**The Wireless Network**	**63**
	Get Started with Wireless Networking	64
	Connect the Hardware	65
	Add a Windows Vista–Based PC	70
	Chapter Summary	75
Chapter 6	**The Network and Sharing Center**	**77**
	Set Up Your Network Locations	78
	Configure Network Discovery	79
	Share Files	80
	Share the Public Folder	81
	Share Printers	82
	Use Password Protection	84
	Share Media	84
	View Computers and Devices	86
	Chapter Summary	88

Part III   Managing the Network   **89**

Chapter 7	**Create User Accounts and Set Parental Controls**	**91**
	Understand User Accounts on the Single PC	92
	Understand User Accounts on the Networked PC	93
	Understand Types of Accounts	93
	Create a User Account with a Password	94
	Set Advanced Account Properties	99
	Set Parental Controls	100
	View Parental Control Reports	103
	Chapter Summary	104
Chapter 8	**Configure and Manage Shared Folders**	**105**
	Create Your Own Shared Folders	106
	Understand Default Permissions	109

Understand Security Permissions   116
Access Shared Folders from a Windows Vista–Based PC   118
Access Shared Folders from a Windows XP–Based PC   119
Chapter Summary   120

Chapter 9   Turn On and Manage Printer Sharing   121

Share a Printer with the Windows Vista Operating System   122
Add Drivers   124
Set Security Permissions   127
Configure Advanced Printer Settings   130
Access a Local Printer   133
Add a Shared Printer Connected to Another PC   135
Chapter Summary   136

Part IV   Expanding the Network   137

Chapter 10   Create a Windows Home Server   139

Understand What Windows Home Server Offers   140
Know the System Requirements   141
Run Windows Home Server Setup   144
Troubleshoot   146
Configure Windows Home Server Settings   149
Manage Windows Home Server   150
Configure the Backup Settings   154
Configure the Windows Home Server Settings   156
View the Home Network Health   158
Explore Additional Features   159
Chapter Summary   159

Chapter 11   Work with Offline Files   161

Understand Offline Files   162
Turn On the Offline Files Feature   162
Select Offline Files   163
Work Offline   165
Learn About Sync Center and Synchronization   166
Use Sync Center and Offline Files   167
Create a Sync Partnership   171
Chapter Summary   172

Chapter 12   **Add an Xbox 360**   **173**

Opt for the Xbox   174
Meet Network Requirements   174
Connect the Xbox 360 to the Network   175
Configure the Xbox 360   175
Configure the Windows Vista–Based PC   176
Understand What Media Can Be Shared   178
Chapter Summary   179

Chapter 13   **Access a Network Remotely**   **181**

Know the System and Network Requirements   182
Create a Virtual Private Network   183
Set Up the Host PC   183
Make the Connection   186
Configure Additional Settings   192
Chapter Summary   196

Chapter 14   **Maintain a Healthy Network**   **197**

Use Windows Security Center   198
Protect Your Computer from Viruses   203
Work with User Account Control   204
Use Windows Update   206
Use Windows Defender   210
Use Windows Firewall   213
Use Windows Backup and Restore Center   215
Take Care of Your Hardware   220
Chapter Summary   222

Part V   Appendix and Glossary   **223**

Appendix   **225**
Glossary   **239**

Index   *251*

What do you think of this book? We want to hear from you!

Microsoft is interested in hearing your feedback so we can continually improve our books and learning resources for you. To participate in a brief online survey, please visit:

www.microsoft.com/learning/booksurvey/

Acknowledgments

I am so happy I was once again given the opportunity to work with Juliana Aldous and the team at Microsoft Press. Everyone is always so awesome to work with, so helpful, and so creative, and I always enjoy the work I do with them. I'd like to thank Juliana specifically for selecting me for this book, Sandra Haynes for getting it off on the right foot, and Melissa von Tschudi-Sutton for staying with me throughout the process. I'd also like to thank Kim Wimpsett, the copy editor, for dotting my i's and crossing my t's. I guess that's a little cliché these days; I suppose Kim mostly kept me from misusing *disk* and *disc* and rambling on in incomplete sentences. I'd like to thank Curt Simmons for being a great editor, too. He was very professional and prompt, short-winded, and not too hard on me when I had a lapse in technical judgment. I'd be honored to work with every one of these people again at any time at all and under any circumstance.

I'd like to thank my career-long agent Neil Salkind, PhD, at Studio B, and the rest of the team there as well. Really, Neil, a special thanks for always having time for me and for putting up with the cat pictures I send of Pico on my keyboard or chasing the mouse cursor on my monitor. That indeed takes someone special! Finally, I have to note that my family is remarkable, as usual, and they quit asking quite some time ago when I might get a "real job." Thanks for being proud and supportive and for celebrating each and every book with me.

INTRODUCTION

BEING CONNECTED through technology is now a part of life. You're probably already connected to others via cell phones, instant messaging, e-mail, and the Internet, and now it's time to make sure your home is connected, too. This book is here to help you with that endeavor and to make sure you plan, create, and ultimately manage the best network possible for you and your family.

WHY THIS BOOK

This book details exactly what you need to know to set up a network and offers the information in an easy-to-understand format with lots of screen shots and step-by-step instructions. It was written specifically for Windows Vista by a Microsoft MVP and Windows Vista and networking expert and was published by Microsoft Press, so you know you're getting the best book possible for setting up and configuring your Windows Vista–based home network. With this book, you'll learn more than how to create any kind of network easily—you'll also learn how to incorporate Windows Vista–added benefits such as Windows Defender, Windows Security Center, the Network and Sharing Center, Windows Firewall, Remote Desktop, and more. It's everything you'll need to create your network and manage it successfully.

WHO THIS BOOK IS FOR

This book is suitable for just about any user, from beginner to intermediate to even a Windows expert. For instance, this book is a good choice for those who know something about Windows operating systems but not much about creating a network. It's also for anyone who already has a wired network and wants to set up a wireless one, and it's even for someone who wants to set up a temporary wired or wireless network for gaming, conferences, or a quick transfer of files. Even Windows experts can get something here, such as learning how to connect remotely to their home PC from a hotel room in another city or state by using Remote Desktop technology.

SPECIAL ELEMENTS IN THIS BOOK

As you work through this book, you'll run across the following special elements that will help you get more from Windows Vista and home networking:

Tips and notes These offer sound advice for getting better performance, better results, and whatever else can be pulled from a given application or task. These suggestions offer guidance for performing tasks more effectively.

Sidebars These are stand-alone sections within the main body of a chapter. The sidebars are related to the chapter's topic but are completely independent of the chapter discussion. They offer additional information you may need to perform a task but do not pertain to everyone. They also offer information regarding the technologies involved in a specific section or chapter.

HOW THIS BOOK IS ORGANIZED

You don't have to read this book from cover to cover; it is organized into parts so you can find what you want easily. For instance, if you want only to set up a Windows Home Server–based PC, you can immediately skip to Chapter 10; if you know you want to set up an Ethernet network and you already have the hardware, you can skip to Chapter 4. However, if you don't know much about home networking, you may want to read the first part, "Getting Started," in its entirety before moving forward.

This book is divided into five parts, described next.

PART I, "GETTING STARTED"

In Part I, you'll learn what Windows Vista offers regarding home networking, why you should create a network, and what types of networks you can choose. You'll also learn what kind of hardware is needed for each network type, the cost, and how easily these items can be installed if necessary. Finally, you'll learn what you should do prior to setting up a network, such as turning on Windows Firewall, connecting to the Internet, and performing related tasks. If you're not familiar with networking configurations and technologies, this part is a must-read!

PART II, "SETTING UP A NETWORK"

In Part II, you'll choose what type of network you want to create (or upgrade to) and physically create the network. You'll become acquainted with the Network and Sharing Center, where you'll turn on network discovery and file sharing. Finally, you'll browse the network and access shared files. If you already know you want to create a direct connection network, read Chapter 3, but skip Chapters 4 and 5. If you know you want an Ethernet network, read Chapter 4, but skip Chapters 3 and 5. If you're settled on a wireless network, read Chapters 4 and 5, but skip Chapter 3. Wireless networks can also have wired connections, so it's important to read Chapter 5 (or at least skim it) on wired networking. (Everyone needs to read Chapter 6 on using the Network and Sharing Center.)

PART III, "MANAGING THE NETWORK"

In Part III, you'll learn tips for managing the network, such as creating user accounts for each network user, creating and managing shared folders, and creating and managing shared printers. Although you don't have to read the chapters in this part in order, it's ultimately best if you do; you'll read each of them carefully.

PART IV, "EXPANDING THE NETWORK"

In Part IV, you'll find various ways to expand and secure your network, including adding a Windows Home Server–based PC, working with offline files, adding a media extender, accessing the network remotely, and, finally, making sure the network is as secure as possible. In this part, you need to read only the chapters that apply to you, although everyone should read Chapter 14 on securing the network.

PART V, "APPENDIX AND GLOSSARY"

In Part V, you'll have access to an appendix and glossary. The appendix offers myriad ways to get more help if you can't find answers to your questions in this book, and the glossary offers a quick way to look up terms you find in this book and elsewhere that you aren't familiar with.

SUPPORT

Every effort has been made to ensure the accuracy of this book and companion content. Microsoft Press provides corrections for books through the Web at the following address:

www.microsoft.com/learning/support/

To connect directly to the Microsoft Knowledge Base and enter a query regarding a question or issue that you may have, go to the following address:

www.microsoft.com/learning/support/search.asp

If you have comments, questions, or ideas regarding the book or companion content or if you have questions that are not answered by querying the Knowledge Base, please send them to Microsoft Press using either of the following methods:

E-mail:

mspinput@microsoft.com

Postal mail:

Microsoft Press
Attn: *Windows Vista: Home Networking* Editor
One Microsoft Way
Redmond, WA 98052-6399

Please note that product support is not offered through the preceding addresses. For support information, please visit the Microsoft Product Support Web site at the following address:

http://support.microsoft.com

PART I

Getting Started

CHAPTER 1

Introduction to Networking

- **Explore networking options**
- **Select a network type**
- **Select network hardware**
- **Learn networking terms**

CONGRATULATIONS on your new (or updated) PC with the Windows Vista operating system! I hope you've had time to explore some of the awesome new features such as Windows Sidebar, Windows Calendar, Windows Photo Gallery, and the Snipping Tool, as well as the new system and security tools including Windows Defender and Windows Firewall. You have more tools to explore, though, including the outstanding new networking tools.

I'm assuming if you're reading this introduction, you must be just about ready to get on with networking! Because Windows Vista offers several options for home and small-office networks and because I want you to be as happy as possible with the network you configure, I'm going to start by introducing the network types from which you can

...That's what this book is about, acquainting you with all of the Windows Vista network features and teaching you how to use those features to create the best network possible.

choose and the types of hardware you'll need. Following that, you'll learn additional networking terms—some that are quite important and some that are important only to networking enthusiasts!

What Windows Vista Offers

If you've never set up a network before, don't worry. Windows Vista offers the Welcome Center and the Network and Sharing Center to help guide you through the process. If you have had some networking experience, are upgrading from a wired to a wireless network, or are simply adding your first Windows Vista–based PC to an existing network, you need not worry either. Windows Vista and this book will help you achieve whatever you desire.

There's a bit more to setting up a network than simply connecting devices, though. You'll need to tell Windows Vista what exactly you want to share and with whom. You'll want to keep private data private, keep public data public, and manage all this data appropriately. You should also create user accounts for everyone who has access to the network, turn on and manage printer sharing, and make sure you've turned on Network Discovery. You may even want to add a media extender, access your computer remotely, or add a Windows Home Server to extend your network.

Of course, all this is up to you—how far you want to take it, that is—but that's what this book is about, acquainting you with all of the Windows Vista network features and teaching you how to use those features to create the best network possible. Let's get on with some network talk then, starting with why you need a network.

Why You Need a Network

If you have more than one PC in your home or office, you really need some kind of network. There are, perhaps, 1,000 reasons why, but for the sake of limiting this book to a reasonable number of pages, I'll list my top 10 reasons here:

- To share information including data, music, pictures, movies, and other media
- To share resources including printers, cameras, and scanners
- To install and use a firewall (such as a router) to protect the network from unwanted incoming data
- To configure access control for each user with a user name and password
- To centralize management by keeping data that is needed by all users on a server or shared hard drive
- To work wirelessly from a laptop in any room of the house (or from the patio or garden)
- To connect to the Internet from any computer on the network
- To play games against other people in your home or on the Internet
- To create a network-wide backup strategy to keep data safe
- To share a calendar for special dates, business meetings, sports practices and games, and doctor and dentist visits

Types of Network Configurations

Once you know you're ready for a network, you have to figure out what kind of network is right for you. You'll likely choose between one of these types: direct connection, Ethernet, and wireless.

NOTE This chapter provides an overview of network configurations. Entire books have been written on each type, and I in no way hope to compete with them here. I provide only a brief introduction to network options, types, and hardware to get you started, and I will expand on these topics as needed throughout this book.

DIRECT CONNECTION

If you have only two computers to network and you trust everyone who has access to those two computers, you might consider a simple direct connection network. This connection type is almost prehistoric, though; it was one of the first ways people networked their PCs and is horribly slow. Even if you have only two PCs, you should consider another method. I'm introducing it here as an option, but it is certainly not the best one.

A direct connection network connects two computers that each perform independently of one another but can and do share data and other information. With this kind of network, you need only your two computers and a single cable. This is a good choice if you don't want to spend much money on hardware, and it may be the only choice if one of the two computers is an older model, for instance, a computer that came preinstalled with Windows 95 or Windows 98. It's also a good choice if you need to share an Internet connection between the two PCs.

NULL MODEM CABLE

A null modem cable was one of the earliest pieces of hardware used to create a home network. The null modem cable connects two computers by using their serial or parallel ports. In the olden days, all computers came with these ports, but now, well, not so much. Newer computers don't usually come with serial ports, although you will still find parallel ports. So if you want to connect two computers by using this method, you'll have to verify you have a serial port on both PCs or a parallel port on both PCs to make the connection.

ETHERNET CROSSOVER CABLE

You can connect two computers directly by using an Ethernet crossover cable. For this method to work, both computers must have a network interface card (NIC). The NICs offer a place to plug in the Ethernet cable and thus connect the two computers. This is a good option for both dial-up and broadband connections to the Internet because data travels quickly to and from each computer, even when only one computer is actually connected to the Internet. The other computer accesses the Internet seamlessly.

> **NOTE** If one computer has a NIC but the other does not, consider a USB-to-Ethernet converter if the PC has a free USB port. You can also install an Ethernet card (which is a type of NIC) or purchase a serial-to-Ethernet converter if the former is not an option.

USB DIRECT LINK

To easily connect two PCs, you may want to try a USB-to-USB direct link cable. Microsoft offers such a cable, and it's called an Easy Transfer cable. Once connected, as long as you've met the other prerequisites (such as having the proper credentials and having sharing turned on), the network configures itself.

INFRARED

With the proper hardware, you can connect two computers by using an infrared signal. Like USB, once connected, as long as you've met the other prerequisites (such as having the proper credentials and having sharing turned on), the network configures itself.

ETHERNET

If you have more than two computers to network and no network in place—or if you already have a wired network with multiple PCs connected by a hub, switch, or router and simply want to add a Windows Vista–based machine to it (and have it be the boss of things)—you should consider Ethernet. This option is widely extensible, meaning you can add computers, printers, and other hardware easily, including backup devices such as external hard drives or a Windows Home Server.

Ethernet networks connect computers by using a hardware device, preferably a router, although you could use a hub or switch (more on the differences later in this chapter). A router, like a hub or switch, has Ethernet ports and can support many computers. You purchase the size router you need. Generally, a six-port router will suffice.

I prefer a router because a router sees every message, query, or data request sent by every computer on the network, and it ensures that the information goes where it's needed and nowhere else. Routers are especially useful when separating two distinct networks, such as the Internet and your own private home network. Routers, being aware of which data should go where and which data should not be passed through, help keep your network safe from Internet threats such as viruses and other attacks.

WIRELESS

Wireless networks are the most awesome networks of all. They aren't too expensive to create, and they're completely extensible. Of course, you'll need fairly new equipment, but if you're running Windows Vista on one or more PCs and you have a couple of Windows XP machines to connect, you probably meet all of the minimum requirements.

Wireless networks use radio waves, just like cell phones and walkie-talkies. To take advantage of this technology, though, each computer in the network must have a wireless transmitter, or you'll have to spend a few extra bucks on a wireless adapter for each wireless-challenged PC. You'll also need a wireless router to connect it all. Laptops generally use a wireless card, while desktops can connect to a wireless network by using a USB adapter or PCI card installed inside the computer. With a wireless network, computers practically discover themselves. If you have the proper hardware and the ability to purchase the required equipment, I suggest you use a wireless network.

Types of Network Hardware

You'll need different hardware for different networks. Understanding what each network type requires can help you decide the network that's right for you. If you've pretty much already decided you want to connect your only two computers by using an Ethernet crossover cable, you won't have to buy much stuff. However, if you have four or five computers and want to go wired or wireless, you'll need a few extra pieces! So, let's spend some time looking at the hardware required for the three types of networks mentioned in this chapter: direct connection, Ethernet, and wireless. You should be able to decide what's best for you by the end of this section.

DIRECT CONNECTION

If you're looking for a fast, easy way to connect two computers and you aren't concerned with network speed or having a router to protect your data, this may be the network for you. There won't be too much expense in setting up a direct connection network either. A null modem cable costs about $10 US. Serial-to-Ethernet converters, if needed, are about $100 US. An Ethernet crossover cable runs about $10–$20 US depending on the length. USB-to-Ethernet converters start at about $20 US. Infrared converters and USB direct cables are equally inexpensive. This is the most basic of networks, though, so don't expect a lot of perks!

ETHERNET

Ethernet networks are quite popular, and they're easy to set up, fast, and reliable. Almost all computers these days come with the required NIC too, and you can purchase Ethernet cables, hubs, switches, and routers at your local computer store and on the Internet. Before you select this option for you network, though, you need to know what each component does, why it's needed, and what it costs.

NICS

A NIC is a PCI card that is installed inside your computer. It can also be an external device in the form of a converter, such as when connecting a PC to an Ethernet network by using a USB-to-Ethernet converter or something similar. To connect your PCs to Ethernet hardware such as a hub, switch, or router, each PC will need a NIC (or a converter). The cost varies, but generally a NIC you install yourself inside a desktop PC costs less than $30 US, and converters are about the same or even less. Prices vary depending on the speed of the NIC and other factors. You get what you pay for!

ETHERNET CABLE

Ethernet cable is inexpensive. You'll want to buy the fastest cable your hardware can support, and for the most part, this is Cat 5 or Cat 6. Although I could spend chapters talking about the technical side of things, including how the cables transmit data, what the wires do and how they're connected, and why Cat 6 is faster than Cat 5, suffice it to say, for now, the newer the technology, the faster the network.

You'll need one Ethernet cable for each computer you want to connect to your network. The cable will need to be long enough to reach from the hub, switch, or router to the PC being connected. Sometimes, this can be quite a long way. Newer houses often come with Ethernet built into the walls, but if you're in an older home, you may have to run it yourself.

HUBS

You have three choices for networking your PCs. One is a hub. Hubs, switches, and routers all look pretty much the same, but they each perform differently and offer different levels of performance and security. A hub is the lowliest of the three and is therefore the least expensive.

Hubs contain multiple Ethernet ports; you may choose to purchase a hub that offers four, six, eight, or even ten ports. Hubs generally copy all incoming data to all other ports on the network. Unfortunately, the data being sent by one port (the sending PC) is almost always needed at only one other port (the receiving PC), so a lot of data is floating around the network that isn't necessary. This slows down the network. In contrast, more expensive hardware reads the destination address of each data packet and sends the data to the correct port, eliminating unnecessary data on the network. The main advantage of using a hub is that it's really simple to set up and configure, and it's just as easy to incorporate an Internet connection. (And, if your Internet connection uses a modem/router, this may be all you need anyway!)

SWITCHES

Switches also contain multiple Ethernet ports; you may choose to purchase a switch that offers four, six, eight, or more ports. A switch filters and forwards data rather than just forwarding data to everyone on the network. A switch uses a technology called *transparent bridging* to send out a broadcast signal to locate where to send the data prior to sending it. Once it knows where to send the data, it sends it. This speeds up the network by reducing how much data is being sent across it. This is much different from a hub, where all data is sent to everyone on the network and then accepted by the intended recipient.

ROUTERS

A router connects two or more networks. A router is the best choice for a home network with a shared Internet connection. A router combines the functions of a hub, switch, and firewall, offering a much better option for keeping your network safe from the bad guys. A router is also much smarter than a hub or switch.

A router determines where data should be sent and the fastest way to get it there prior to sending it. It does this by keeping a table of the fastest routes from one point to another, so network speed is enhanced. It is believed that routers provide better protection against hackers than software firewalls do, because Internet Protocol (IP) addresses are never exposed directly to the Internet. This makes scanning the local network impossible. Routers are available for wired or wireless networks.

You will already have a broadband router if you have a broadband connection to the Internet. A broadband router means two or more computers can share an Internet connection. A broadband router connects your network to the Internet with only a single IP address. You can purchase a basic broadband router for about $70 US.

> **NOTE** When purchasing any type of hub, switch, or router, always get one with a few more ports than you think you'll need. You never know when you may need to add another computer to your network.

WIRELESS

Wireless is the way to go. It creates security issues to worry about, such as whether your neighbor can access your wireless network or Internet connection, but if set up properly, this shouldn't be an issue. Wireless hardware is inexpensive too, and once you get past the router setup, which may take a bit of time, the ability to work anywhere within the range of the wireless router far outweighs the time spent.

WIRELESS ADAPTERS

For a computer to connect to a wireless network, the computer will need a wireless adapter. If you have a newer computer, one may be built in. If you have older computers or low-end models, you'll need to purchase an external wireless adapter that connects via USB, purchase a wireless adapter card (for a laptop), or purchase and install a wireless adapter PCI card inside the PC itself.

> **NOTE** If you have a computer that does not have a wireless adapter and you can't afford one, you can physically connect the PC to the wireless router's available Ethernet ports.

ROUTERS

A wireless network contains a wireless router. The router connects the PCs on the network and also connects to your digital subscriber line (DSL) or cable modem. You can use the wireless router along with a broadband connection to share an Internet connection with everyone on the network. Even the slowest wireless routers are often faster than cable or DSL, so the wireless router will not slow down your Web surfing speed.

Loads of wireless router technologies exist, and I'll briefly summarize them next, although now is not the place for such technical talk (this is Chapter 1, after all!). When you purchase your wireless router, just make sure it's compatible with your wireless adapters and access points. Get the latest technology you can afford, and talk to the salespeople.

Here's a short rundown of wireless technologies:

- Wireless data transmits at frequencies of 2.4 gigahertz (GHz) or 5 GHz and uses 802.11 networking standards.
- 802.11b was the first version. It is the slowest and least expensive.
- 802.11g is newer and faster, but even faster versions are on the horizon. For now, 801.11g is the most popular.
- 802.11a transmits at 5 GHz but isn't widely used.
- 802.11n is the fastest and will soon become standard.

ACCESS POINTS

Wireless access points (WAPs) are additional pieces of hardware on a wireless network that act as transmitters and receivers of wireless signals. Generally, they are small hardware devices with built-in network adapters, antennas, and radio transmitters. Newer access points can support 255 computers! You will learn more about WAPs in Chapter 5.

Additional Network Terms to Know

I've only skimmed the surface with regard to networks, network configurations, network hardware, and network technologies, but that's all you need to know to get started. As you continue to work through the book, you'll learn much more about everything introduced in this chapter. However, for the sake of making sure no important term goes without introduction, here are few words you should know:

Broadband Any connection to the Internet that is faster than dial-up. This includes DSL and cable.

Broadband transmission The speed at which data can be transmitted across the network. Generally, the newer the technology, the faster the transmission.

Category 5 (Cat 5) cable A type of cabling commonly used in Ethernet networks to connect computers to network hardware.

Domain Name System (DNS) The system that translates friendly Web site names such as *www.microsoft.com* into their associated IP addresses. Internet sites are located by using their IP addresses, and this system keeps a list of all names and addresses throughout the world.

Ethernet A local area network (LAN) protocol that employs Cat cables to transmit data. Ethernet runs at speeds of 10 megabits per second (Mbps), 100 Mbps, and 1000 Mbps.

Firewall A software or hardware-software combination that protects a private network from attacks and unauthorized access from the Internet.

IP address A unique number given to every computer that accesses the Internet. An Internet service provider (ISP) provides your unique number each time you log on to the Internet.

LAN A network confined to a home or office, such as the network you will create by using this book.

Modem A device that lets digital data be transmitted along analog telephone lines.

Port Connections you'll find on the back of your computer and on hubs, switches, and routers.

Transmission Control Protocol/Internet Protocol (TCP/IP) A set of rules defining how data is exchanged over the Internet.

Wide area network (WAN) A larger network such as one for a large organization that spans a city, state, or country. This term is also used to describe the Internet.

BEFORE PURCHASING THE EQUIPMENT

Before you head out to the local computer store and start buying equipment, take some time to really consider what you want. You need to make a firm decision about the type of network that will suit your needs before buying anything.

LOWEST COST

If you're looking to spend as little as possible, take inventory of what you already have. Do all your computers have NICs but none has a wireless adapter? Ethernet will cost less to set up. But if all your computers have wireless adapters except one or two, a wireless network may be less expensive. Additionally, if you already have a broadband router protecting the network, you may need only a hub to share that connection with other computers.

LATEST TECHNOLOGY

If you want the fastest and most secure network possible, you're going to need to purchase the latest equipment. You won't be able to purchase a 10-Mbps NIC for each of your PCs and connect them with a 100-Mbps router and think you're going to get the best performance possible. If you want performance and speed, make sure you spend the money necessary, get compatible hardware, and get the latest offerings.

WIRED OR WIRELESS

If you even think you *might* want to surf the Internet while sitting on your patio, you owe it to yourself to go wireless from the start. If you don't mind being physically connected and you always work on or access your computer from a single room or desk, by all means stick with Ethernet if you want.

I WANT IT ALL!

If you want it all, I suggest a wireless network combined with a broadband connection to the Internet. Wireless routers let you connect by using Ethernet if you need to, just in case you have guests who bring their own computers that do not have wireless adapters or in case you want to connect an older PC that can't be upgraded. Wireless is not quite as secure as wired, though; even with all the improvements in wireless technology, there's still a chance someone could hack into your personal network. When setting up your wireless network, take every possible precaution to secure it.

IMPORTANT If you think you know what type of network you want to set up, browse through the corresponding chapters before purchasing any new equipment.

Chapter Summary

In this chapter, you learned quite a bit about networking, including why you need a network, what types of networks are available, and what hardware you'll need to create them. You also learned a handful of networking terms to help get you started on the road to networking.

CHAPTER 2

Get Ready!

- **Configure your Windows Vista–based PC for the best performance**
- **Use and understand User Account Control**
- **Configure Windows Firewall and Windows Defender**
- **Consider additional security measures**

ALTHOUGH I'm sure you're ready to start plugging in cables and configuring routers, let's take a few minutes to make sure your Windows Vista–based PC is fully ready to protect the network you want to set up, including but not limited to your personal data, your family and friends' data, and your own PC's health.

In this chapter, you'll configure your PC for an easier initial network setup by connecting printers, connecting to the Internet, and turning on Windows Update. After that, you'll learn about the new User Account Control feature, Windows Firewall, Windows Defender, and the optional feature Windows Live OneCare. Then you'll be ready to start putting the network together.

Configure Your Windows Vista–Based PC

...If you can manage your shared hardware from one PC, specifically a Windows Vista–based PC, you'll have more control over what happens with it, such as who can print to certain printers and when.

It's best to have everything in order before creating a network or adding computers to an existing one. This means connecting everything you want to share and turning on features that will protect your computer (and thus the network) for the long term.

CONNECT PRINTERS

You may already have a printer or two connected to an existing computer in your home. If you've brought in a new Windows Vista–based PC, though, and are creating a network, it's best to start fresh and (re)connect the printer(s) to this newer machine (or the one just upgraded to Windows Vista). The reasoning behind this is that with the printers and other shared devices connected to a single Windows Vista–based PC, you can manage the printers and any other shared devices from one place. You also gain the ability to apply the new security features of Windows Vista to the printer, as well as having easy access to your hardware. It would be a shame to have a network with four computers but have to manage one printer from Windows Vista and another printer from an older Windows 98–based PC.

You might have good reason to leave printers, scanners, and other hardware where they are, though. If the hardware is more accessible and better suited where it is, leave it there. The point is that if you can manage your shared hardware from one PC, specifically a Windows Vista–based PC, you'll have more control over what happens with it, such as who can print to certain printers and when.

You'll connect your printer to your Windows Vista–based PC the same way you connected it previously to any other computer in your home. First locate the driver disk that came with the printer, and reread the instructions. Depending on the printer, you may need to install the driver before plugging in and turning on the printer (and this may prompt you to visit the manufacturer's Web site and download the driver for Windows Vista). For the most part, though, printers connect via USB ports, and once they're connected, plugged in, and turned on, Windows Vista will recognize and install them automatically. It has been my experience that 99 percent of the time, no driver disk is necessary, and no intervention is required from the user.

CONNECT TO THE INTERNET

During network setup, if a connection to the Internet is present, it will be incorporated into the network and shared with other networked computers. So, it's best to connect to the Internet prior to setting up any network or running any network wizards.

If you're using a dial-up connection, consider moving that connection to the Windows Vista–based PC. Windows Vista offers new enhancements such as Windows Defender, not available in other operating systems, that will help protect the network from Internet ills. Windows Defender also scans the computer regularly, so it makes sense to run any connection from Windows Vista where possible.

Many people no longer use dial-up, though. Broadband is becoming the norm, and wireless Internet is not far behind. With these types of connections, usually a router is involved, and in this scenario, the router provides protection. Often there's another piece of equipment too, such as a hub, that connects all computers on the network to the broadband router or access points on wireless computers. If that's the case, you don't need to move any existing equipment. However, it's still important to use Windows Update, Windows Defender, and Windows Firewall to get the best protection possible.

CONFIGURE WINDOWS UPDATE

Windows Update provides updates to the operating system and related components, including definition updates for Windows Defender, drivers for connected hardware, and Junk Mail filter updates for Windows Mail. Technically, an *update* is a patch or full file replacement for software that is already installed on a computer. Windows Update also contains updates for the Microsoft Office system, offers Windows Ultimate Extras, and offers critical security updates for recently discovered security holes in the operating system. It's best to turn on Windows Update and let it run on its own; however, you can turn on Windows Update and manage and install the updates yourself, thereby controlling what does and does not get installed.

TURN ON WINDOWS UPDATE

You can access Windows Update settings in two ways. One way is to click Start, and in the Start Search box, type **Windows Update**. As shown in Figure 2-1, Windows Update will be listed under Programs. You can also click Start, then click All Programs, and finally click Windows Update.

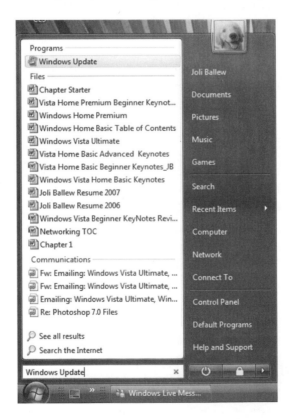

Figure 2-1 The easiest way to access Windows Update settings is to type **Windows Update** in the Start Search box on the Start menu.

Once the Windows Update window is open, follow these steps:

1. Click Change Settings.

2. In the Change Settings window, change how and when you want Windows Vista to obtain updates. Figure 2-2 shows the recommended settings. Select from the following:

   • Install Updates Automatically (Recommended)

   • Download Updates But Let Me Choose Whether To Install Them

   • Check For Updates But Let Me Choose Whether To Download And Install Them

   • Never Check For Updates (Not Recommended)

3. Select or deselect Include Recommended Updates When Downloading, Installing, Or Notifying Me About Updates.

4. Under Update Service, select or deselect Use Microsoft Update.

5. Click OK.

TIP Make sure when selecting a time to install updates that the computer will be on at that time and, preferably, idle.

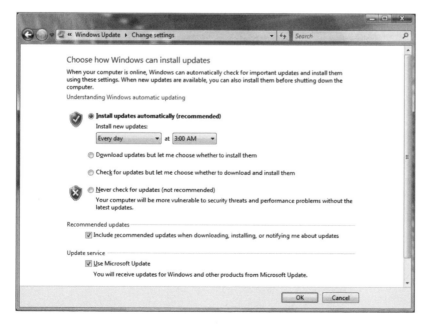

Figure 2-2
It's best to configure Windows Update settings similarly to what's shown here.

INSTALL OPTIONAL UPDATES

You can view and install optional updates from Windows Update. Figure 2-3 shows a computer with several optional updates. To view the updates, click View Available Updates, denoted here with a box around it.

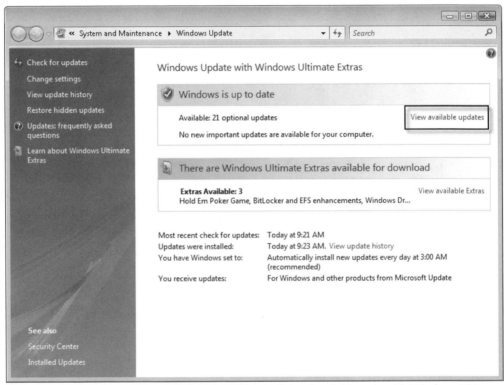

Figure 2-3 Optional updates and Windows Ultimate Extras (available only with Windows Vista Ultimate) are not installed by default; you select what to install.

Figure 2-4 shows the optional updates for a sample Windows Vista–based PC. I've selected the Windows Vista updates only. Because these updates are optional, you can install any or all of them. It's your choice.

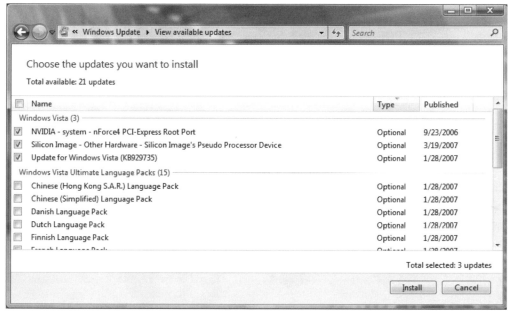

Figure 2-4 You choose which, if any, optional updates to install.

TURN ON USER ACCOUNT CONTROL

User Account Control helps prevent unauthorized changes to your computer by potentially dangerous software and code. User Account Control works with Windows Defender as well as Windows Internet Explorer 7 in Windows Vista to help reduce your chances that viruses, spyware, or other Internet threats will attack and install on your PCs. With User Account Control, standard users are prompted for administrator credentials when they try to install most programs, change system settings, and perform similar tasks. Even when logged on as an administrator, you'll see User Account Control offers a higher level of security than ever before by prompting you to continue after verifying the application is from a known source.

By default, User Account Control is turned on. To verify it's on or to turn it off (which I don't recommend), follow these steps:

1. Click Start, and click Control Panel.

2. Click User Accounts And Family Safety.

3. Click User Accounts.

4. Click Turn User Account Control On Or Off.

5. Verify Use User Account Control (UAC) To Help Protect Your Computer is selected.

6. Click OK.

Configure Windows Firewall

Windows Firewall can stop most Internet threats before they infect your computer and network and is turned on by default. The firewall examines data that comes into and goes out of your computer via a network (or port) and allows it if it's authorized and blocks it if it's unauthorized. You can configure what's allowed and blocked by tweaking the firewall settings. You have two Windows Firewall options: Windows Firewall and Windows Firewall with Advanced Security. You'll want to familiarize yourself with both.

PICK WINDOWS FIREWALL

You access Windows Firewall by opening Control Panel and clicking Security. In Security, you can turn the firewall on or off, and you can allow a specific program to move through the firewall uninterrupted. You'll want to leave the firewall turned on (unless you've installed a third-party firewall), and you'll probably need to turn on exceptions to allow certain data, such as file and print sharing to move through the firewall automatically.

To turn on Windows Firewall and configure exceptions for programs you use often, follow these steps:

1. Open Control Panel.

2. Click Windows Firewall.

3. Click Change Settings.

4. On the General tab, verify On (Recommended) is selected. You can choose a different option, but this is the recommended setting.

5. On the Exceptions tab, browse through the list, and select the programs you want to allow through the firewall. Several are probably already selected. Some options you may want to consider include the following:

   a. File And Printer Sharing

   b. Remote Desktop

   c. Windows Media Player

   d. Windows Media Player Sharing Service

6. On the Advanced tab, select the network connections to protect. (They are probably already selected.)

7. Click OK.

PICK WINDOWS FIREWALL WITH ADVANCED SECURITY

Windows Firewall with Advanced Security provides even more security for Windows computers that are on a network. The easiest way to access these settings is from the Start menu. Type **Windows Firewall**, and select Windows Firewall With Advanced Security to open the window shown in Figure 2-5.

As shown in Figure 2-5, you can see an overview of the advanced security settings for the profiles configured on your computer. What you see may differ from what's shown here.

With this application, not only can you configure security locally, but you can also configure firewall settings for remote computers by using group policies. Firewall settings are integrated with Internet Protocol security (IPsec). You can configure these settings for computers in domains or those connected to private or public networks. You should not tinker with these settings or change anything here unless you are extremely sure of what you are doing because you might disable the network or create problems that will be difficult to diagnose and resolve later.

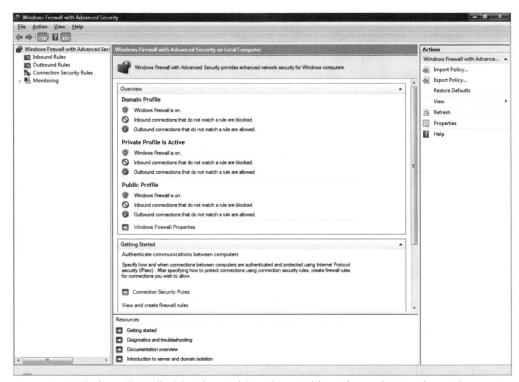

Figure 2-5 Windows Firewall with Advanced Security provides enhanced network security.

Configure Windows Defender

Windows Defender is the last feature to tackle before plugging in any network computers or reconfiguring an existing network. Windows Defender is an always-on security feature that offers real-time protection against spyware and other unwanted software. It also scans the computer regularly, by default, in search of software that might have slipped past the Windows Vista defenses. With Windows Defender, you control everything, from how and when scanning occurs to what to do when problems are found.

Once again, this feature is available by opening Control Panel and then clicking Security. Figure 2-6 shows Windows Defender; this computer has been scanned recently, and Windows Defender didn't detect any harmful software.

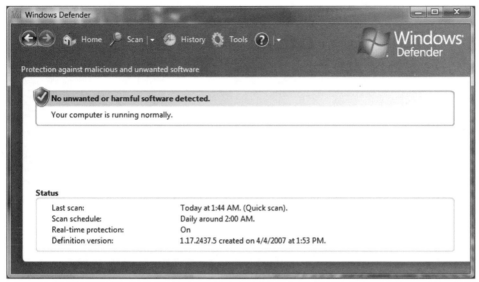

Figure 2-6 This is what you'd like to see when opening Windows Defender.

VERIFY WINDOWS DEFENDER IS WORKING

To view the status of your computer and determine whether Windows Defender is on or to turn it on if it is not running, follow these steps:

1. Open Control Panel, and click Security.

2. Click Windows Defender. If you see something similar to what's shown in Figure 2-6, Windows Defender is turned on and running in the background. If Windows Defender is not on, follow these steps:

   a. Click Tools.

   b. Under Settings, click Options.

   c. Scroll down to Administrator Options, and select Use Windows Defender and Allow Everyone To Use Windows Defender.

3. Click Save, and close the Windows Defender window.

CONFIGURE WINDOWS DEFENDER

You can configure several options in Windows Defender, including when and how to scan for harmful software and what to do with quarantined items. For the most part, the defaults are probably fine; however, it never hurts to browse through the options to become familiar with what's available.

CONFIGURE TOOLS

Tools is an option in Windows Defender and, when selected, offers the choices shown in Figure 2-7. Each option is briefly detailed next.

Figure 2-7 Use Tools and Settings to configure how, when, where, and why Windows Defender functions.

Options Here you can set up automatic scanning and configure the frequency, time, and type of scan (quick or full). You can also choose to look for updated definitions prior to scanning and apply default actions to items detected during a scan. Also available are options to configure default actions of your own for high-alert, medium-alert, and low-alert items. It's recommended you turn on real-time protection for Auto Start, System Configuration, Internet Explorer Add-Ons, Internet Explorer Downloads, Services And Drivers, and more. Finally, you'll see advanced options such as creating a restore point prior to every scan and selecting files or locations you do not want to scan.

Microsoft SpyNet Join Microsoft SpyNet, an online community, where members help you choose how you want to respond to software threats found by Windows Defender. You can select a basic or advanced membership. Membership is free.

Quarantined Items View quarantined items, and choose to restore them, remove them, or ignore them.

Software Explorer View the applications running on your computer, and see whether they are being permitted or blocked. You can filter the programs list to view only Startup programs, currently running programs, network-connected programs, or Winsock service providers. Select any program to obtain information about it, including the file name, the publisher, and even whether the driver is digitally signed. Click End Process to stop any running application.

Allowed Items View allowed items. These are items Windows Defender has determined might be harmful but you've allowed anyway. You can select any item and remove it.

Windows Defender Website Select to visit the Windows Defender Web site where you can learn more about Windows Defender, including signing up for newsletters, downloading the latest security updates, accessing support and training materials, and more.

USE SCAN AND HISTORY

Scan and History are two additional options for Windows Defender. Scan lets you perform a quick scan or a full scan anytime you want. Custom scans are also available, if you want to perform a scan on a particular file or folder (such as a download or a CD or DVD from an unknown source).

History is available so you can view all Windows Defender activities. This includes the programs you've allowed to run and their names and alert levels.

WINDOWS LIVE ONECARE

Windows Live OneCare runs in the background to protect your PC from viruses, spyware, hackers, and other Internet intruders. It also automatically backs up your important files, cleans up and tunes your PC, and keeps it running as well as possible. Currently, Microsoft is offering a 90-day free trial.

UNDERSTAND WHAT WINDOWS LIVE ONECARE OFFERS

Windows Live OneCare offers antivirus software, antispyware software, antiphishing software, a two-way firewall, performance tune-ups, and backup and restore features. These features block most Internet threats from ever getting on your computer, remove harmful software if it does get past Windows Live OneCare, protect against pop-ups, block harmful applications, automatically defragment disks, clean and compress temporary files, and install operating system updates.

DOWNLOAD WINDOWS LIVE ONECARE

You can access Windows Live OneCare from the Welcome Center. Just open the Welcome Center from the Start menu, click Go Online To Help Protect Your PC With Windows Live, and click Learn More Online. The Windows Live home page will open automatically in Internet Explorer 7. To get Windows Live OneCare, simply look for the Get It link.

Chapter Summary

In this chapter, you learned how to configure your Windows Vista–based PC for best performance, first by connecting everything you want to share on the network but mainly by verifying security measures are in place and tweaking how the available security applications work. This included Windows Update, Windows Firewall, Windows Defender, and a few extras such as Windows Live OneCare.

PART II   Setting Up a Network

CHAPTER 3

The Direct Connection Network

- **Choose a workgroup name**
- **Physically connect two PCs by using one of several methods**
- **Turn on the network**
- **Share an Internet connection**

THE MOST BASIC TYPE of network is one consisting of only two computers connected directly to each other via a single cable. For older PCs, that cable is often a serial null modem cable or a parallel interlink cable. For newer PCs, it's a direct Ethernet cable, also referred to as a patch or crossover cable, a USB link cable, or a FireWire cable. If you have the proper hardware installed, you can even make the connection by using an infrared connection, with no wires at all!

In this chapter, you'll learn how to set up a direct connection network and how to share an Internet connection between them. Once the network is up and running, skip to Chapter 6 to configure the network.

Create Workgroup Names

The most basic type of network is one consisting of only two computers connected directly to each other via a single cable.

A workgroup contains two or more computers that are connected to each other for the purpose of sharing data, hardware, and connectivity to the Internet. For two computers to be able to communicate effectively, both need to be members of the same workgroup. So, before moving forward, create a workgroup name for both PCs you'll connect.

CREATE A WORKGROUP NAME ON WINDOWS VISTA

To create a workgroup name (and see the default workgroup name) on your Windows Vista–based PC, follow these steps:

1. Click Start, right-click Computer, and click Properties.

2. Under Computer Name, Domain, And Workgroup Settings, click Change Settings. Click Continue when the UAC alert appears.

3. The default name of the workgroup is Workgroup. To change this to something else, click Change.

4. In Workgroup, type a new name. Click OK.

5. Click OK to close. Restart your computer if prompted to do so.

CREATE A WORKGROUP NAME ON WINDOWS XP

To create a workgroup name (and see the default workgroup name) on your Windows XP–based PC, follow these steps:

1. Click Start, right-click My Computer, and click Properties.

2. On the Computer Name tab, click Change.

3. In Workgroup, type a new name. Click OK.

4. Click OK to close. Restart your computer if prompted to do so.

Physically Connect the Two PCs

A direct cable connection is a physical link between two computers using a single cable (or using an infrared connection) instead of an intermediate piece of hardware such as a modem, hub, switch, or router. You can make this connection a number of ways, but for the most part, physically connecting two PCs is as simple as inserting the required cable into the proper port at the back of each computer. There's only one way to connect them.

Here's an example: If you're using an Ethernet patch cable, you'll plug one end of the Ethernet patch cable into one PC's Ethernet port, and you'll plug the other end into the other PC's Ethernet port. For a USB link cable, you'll connect the PCs through their USB ports. If it's a serial or parallel null modem cable, it's the same type of connection.

No matter what type of connection you make, there's a good chance you'll see a pop-up in the Notification area of one or both PCs, as shown in Figure 3-1. In this particular instance, a local network is found, but an Internet connection is not. Here, two computers are connected directly to each other, but neither is connected to the Internet.

Figure 3-1 Once a physical connection is made, Windows Vista will attempt to configure the connection.

Figure 3-2 shows a different scenario. Here, the PCs are connected via their Ethernet ports. The Windows Vista–based PC has two Ethernet ports; one Ethernet port connects an existing connection to the Internet, and the other Ethernet port connects to the second PC via an Ethernet patch cable. You may see something like this if one PC is connected to the Internet via a cable modem, dial-up connection, or satellite access through one port and connected to a PC through a second port.

Figure 3-2 You may see more than one network.

The hardware you choose to connect the two computers defines what you have to do on the PCs to get them to share their data. If you're using an older technology, such as a parallel null modem cable, you'll have more work ahead of you than if you simply connect via USB or Ethernet. In general, the newer the technology, the easier it is to set up.

> **NOTE** Just because the PC that connects to the Internet can access the Internet does not mean the second PC is able to access it or that it can access the first PC's files. You'll need to turn on network discovery and tell Windows Vista what you do and do not want to share to turn on the network.

Turn On Network Discovery on the Windows Vista–Based PC

As noted, although you may see a pop-up on the Windows Vista–based machine (which I'll call the *host*) or your second PC (which I'll call the *guest*) stating that a network has been found and you're connected, you still need to work through a set series of steps to set up the network. This is important because you must turn on network discovery and establish what you want to share on every Windows Vista–based PC.

On each Windows Vista–based computer, follow these steps:

1. Click Start, click Control Panel, and then click Network And Internet.

2. Under Network And Sharing Center, click Set Up File Sharing.

3. As shown in Figure 3-3, network discovery is off by default. To turn it on, click the down arrow by Network Discovery, and select Turn On Network Discovery, as shown in Figure 3-4.

4. Click Apply.

5. Click Continue to verify you want to turn on network discovery.

6. When prompted whether to turn on network discovery for all public networks, select No.

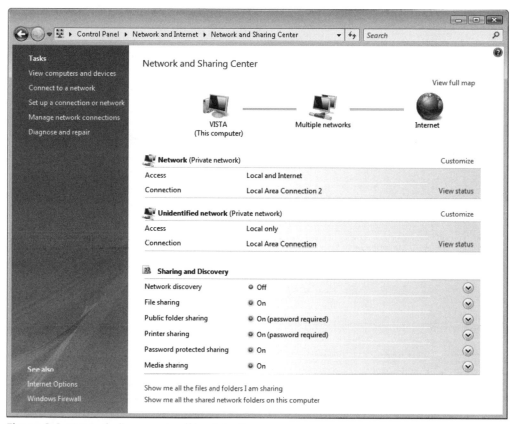

Figure 3-3 Network discovery is off by default.

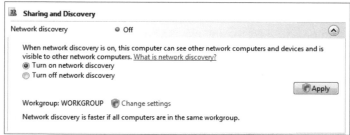

Figure 3-4 Turn on network discovery so you can view and access the second computer and its shared data.

You should now be able to view the two computers on the network by clicking Start and then Network. Figure 3-5 shows a sample network. In this example, VISTA is the host computer (and also offers shared media), and LAPTOP is the guest.

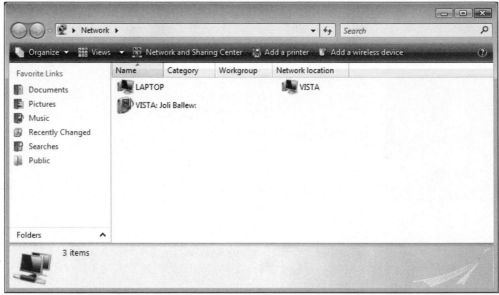

Figure 3-5 Once network sharing is turned on for the Windows Vista–based PCs, you can see and access the networked PC and the Internet.

Share the Host's Internet Connection

After successfully turning on network discovery on the Windows Vista–based PC, you'll want to share that PC's connection to the Internet so the second PC can use it to get online. To share the host's Internet connection, follow these steps:

1. Click Start, and click Network.

2. Click Network And Sharing Center.

3. Click Manage Network Connections.

4. Right-click the connection used to connect to the Internet, and click Properties. Click Continue on the UAC alert.

5. Click the Sharing tab if you have a dial-up connection.

6. Select Allow Other Network Users To Connect Through This Computer's Internet Connection. If desired, deselect Allow Other Network Users To Control Or Disable The Shared Internet Connections.

7. Click OK.

Add a Second Windows Vista–Based PC

If the second PC is running Windows Vista and you're connected via USB, Ethernet, or infrared, you will be automatically prompted to set up the network. In the window that appears regarding what type of network you want to connect to, click Home, and then click Continue. Close the window.

If for some reason you are not prompted, first make sure you're using the proper cable connection. If you're using Ethernet, remember that the cable needs to be a patch cable, not a regular Ethernet cable. If you're sure the cable is the correct one but you still aren't prompted, then restart the computer. If necessary, you may have to turn on network discovery manually to complete the connection process. As noted earlier, you do this in the Network and Sharing Center. It has been my experience that 99 percent of the time, you're prompted with the appropriate options.

Add a Windows XP–Based PC

If you need to connect a Windows XP computer to a PC running Windows Vista, first turn on network discovery on the Windows Vista–based PC and then share the Internet connection as detailed earlier.

After that, choose the installation option for the type of connection you've made:

- Serial or parallel null modem cable
- Ethernet crossover cable
- USB or a Windows Easy Transfer cable
- Infrared

NOTE Bluetooth technology supports wireless connections between computers without the need for additional network hardware, if both computers have Bluetooth capability. Bluetooth works best when a computer is paired with a smaller device—such as a phone, personal digital assistant (PDA), or handheld computer—and if both are physically close. I do not suggest this as a long-term networking strategy for two PCs and, therefore, won't discuss it here.

NULL MODEM CABLE OR PARALLEL INTERLINK CABLE

On a guest PC running Windows XP, you'll need to perform the following steps to make a direct cable connection via a null modem cable or a parallel interlink cable:

1. Click Start, click Control Panel, and click Network Connections.

2. Under Network Tasks, click Create New Connection, and click Next.

3. Click Set Up An Advanced Connection, and click Next.

4. Select Connect Directly To Another Computer, and click Next.

5. Choose the role this computer will play in the network. For this example, select Guest. Click Next.

6. Type the name of the other PC in the box when prompted. Click Next.

7. Select the communication method. For a parallel cable, select LPT1. Click Next. Click Finish.

8. When prompted, type the user name and password you use to access your Windows Vista–based computer. If you do not have a password-protected user account on the Windows Vista–based PC, follow the instructions in the "Create a Password-Protected Account" sidebar, and return here to log on with that account.

ETHERNET CROSSOVER CABLE

If you've set up the host running Windows Vista by turning on network discovery, sharing the Internet connection, and verifying the workgroup names are the same for both PCs, the Ethernet direct connection network will automatically connect.

USB OR A WINDOWS EASY TRANSFER CABLE

If you've set up the host running Windows Vista by turning on network discovery, sharing the Internet connection, and verifying the workgroup names are the same for both PCs, the USB direct connection network will automatically connect.

INFRARED

With infrared technology, computers and other devices can communicate by using short-range wireless signals, provided both have infrared capabilities. With infrared, computers transfer data bidirectionally. The technology is similar to what's used in remote controls for televisions and DVD players. Although infrared adapters are installed in lots of laptops and handheld devices, you don't find them nearly as often in PCs. However, you can add the technology. The easiest way is to purchase a USB-to-infrared converter.

In Windows, you create infrared connections the same way you create other LAN connections. This is a good option if you need to connect two computers temporarily to exchange data with another PC quickly.

The problem with this type of network is that it spans very short distances. The computers need to be within a few feet of each other. Network signals cannot go through walls, and they work only in the direct line of sight.

If you've set up the host running Windows Vista by turning on network discovery, sharing the Internet connection, and verifying the workgroup names are the same for both PCs, you'll then configure the infrared connection by using the same process outlined in the "Null Modem Cable or Parallel Interlink Cable" section earlier. This time, though, you'll select infrared for the connection type, as shown in Figure 3-6.

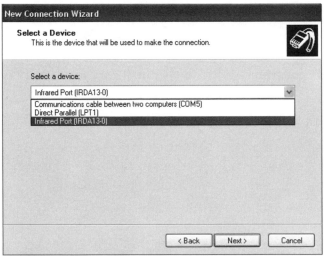

Figure 3-6 Once network sharing is turned on and the Internet connection is shared, select a network type.

CREATE A PASSWORD-PROTECTED ACCOUNT

To access the Windows Vista–based PC from another computer, you must have a password-protected account on the Windows Vista–based PC, and you must use that account to log on each time you're prompted. To create a password-protected account on your Windows Vista–based PC, follow these steps:

1. Click Start, click Control Panel, and click Add Or Remove User Accounts. Click Continue.

2. Decide whether you want to add a password to your account or create a new one. If your account is an administrator account, create a password for it anyway. Then, decide whether you want to use that account for logging in across the network or whether you'd rather use a standard account. I suggest you create a new, standard password-protected account. You'll learn more about that in Chapter 7.

3. To add a password to an existing account that does not have one, follow these steps:

   a. Double-click your account, and select Create A Password.

   b. Type the new password, confirm it, and create a password hint.

   c. Click Create Password.

4. To create a new standard account and create a password for it, follow these steps:

   a. Click Create New Account.

   b. Type a name for the user account.

   c. Select Standard User.

   d. Click Create Account.

   e. Select the new account, and work through step 3 in this procedure.

5. Close the User Accounts window.

Get Help for Networking Older PCs

If you need to connect an older PC, such as one running Windows 2000 or Windows ME, you can follow the directions noted in this chapter. Although the tabs or windows might be a bit different, for the most part the process is the same. Connecting a Windows 98–based PC requires quite a bit more doing, and although I do not have space here to work through all the steps, the support pages at *www.microsoft.com* offer a lot of information. To locate the information you need, go to *http://support .microsoft.com*, and in the search box, type **814235**. This is the first part of a multi-part article for working with Windows 98 in a workgroup setting.

Chapter Summary

In this chapter, you learned how to physically connect two computers and set up a network between them. You learned you have multiple ways to connect PCs, including Ethernet, null modem, USB, FireWire, and infrared. There are also different requirements for connecting computers running Windows Vista, Windows XP, and older operating systems.

CHAPTER 4

The Wired Ethernet Network

- **Connect the hardware**
- **Understand the hardware's boot order**
- **Personalize your network**
- **Turn on the network and share an Internet connection**
- **Add PCs or a Mac**

ETHERNET is a widely used networking technology and is one of the easiest to physically connect. The physical connection involves plugging in a hub, switch, or router and then connecting the PC with Ethernet cables. If you have a broadband modem, the router is positioned (virtually) between it and the PCs.

The speed that data is transferred across the network depends on the hardware you own and purchase. Older Ethernet cards transmit data at 10 Mbps; fast Ethernet transmits at 100 Mbps; and Gigabit Ethernet transmits at 1 gigabit per second (Gbps), that is, 1 billion bits per second. If you're planning to purchase new equipment, keep this in mind. One older 10-Mbps NIC can certainly slow down network data transfer, even with the best equipment.

Ethernet is a widely used networking technology and is one of the easiest to physically connect.

In this chapter, you'll learn how to physically connect two or more PCs by using Ethernet technology. You'll also learn what to do with the broadband modem you use to connect to the Internet. Once configured, you'll be able share your Internet connection with all the computers on the network.

Connect the Hardware

Take inventory of all the hardware you've purchased and you own. You should have a hub, switch, or router and possibly a cable, DSL, or satellite modem. You'll also have an Ethernet cable for connecting each computer. You'll have two types of setup options as well: one that includes a broadband modem and one that does not.

CONNECT A CABLE, DSL, OR SATELLITE MODEM

If you have an external modem (cable, DSL, satellite) and you are not sure whether it's connected properly or need to reinstall it, this section shows you how to connect it. For the most part, this won't be necessary because if you already use a modem, it'll already be set up and configured.

To set up a broadband modem, follow these steps:

1. Connect the modem to the PC with the Windows Vista operating system. You can make the connection by using a USB or Ethernet port. For security reasons, connecting with Ethernet is the better choice.

2. Connect the modem to the cable outlet in the wall, and verify it's connected to a power outlet. Turn on the modem. Insert the CD that came with your modem, and follow the installation instructions.

3. Verify the proper lights are blinking or lit on the modem before continuing.

CONNECT A HUB, SWITCH, OR ROUTER

Physically connecting a hub or switch usually doesn't require a lot of effort. For the most part, it's as simple as inserting the Ethernet cables properly. Installing a router is a bit more complex and requires you to carefully follow the directions that came with it. So before you get started, read the documentation that came with your hardware, and then continue to the next section.

HUBS AND SWITCHES

Hubs and switches are generally plug and play, which means you can connect the hub or switch, install any device drivers that came with it, and then plug in your PCs without any additional configuration required.

To install a hub or switch, follow these steps:

1. Turn on your Windows Vista–based PC, and log on with an administrator account.

2. Connect the hub or switch to a power supply, and turn it on.

3. Look at the hardware panel for blinking lights. The hub will perform several self-tests. Read any documentation that came with the hub before continuing.

4. Connect the hub to the PC via Ethernet. When connecting, make sure you use the hub's Ethernet port marked 1, 2, 3, 4, or another number. Do not connect by using the wide area network (WAN) port on the hub or switch; that's to connect your cable modem.

5. If prompted, insert the driver disc that came with the hub or switch. This may not be necessary, because Windows Vista may install the hub automatically.

6. Verify the light is on at the hub for the Ethernet port you used to connect the PC. You'll add other PCs by connecting them to the hub or switch.

To include a cable, DSL, or satellite modem, follow these steps:

1. Perform the steps for installing the hub or switch as detailed in the previous example.

2. Turn off the PC and hub or switch.

3. Connect the hub to the modem with an Ethernet cable. From the modem, select the Ethernet port. From the hub or switch, select WAN. If the modem's Ethernet port is being used to connect directly to a PC, disconnect it from both the PC and the modem.

4. Turn on the cable, DSL, or satellite modem. Wait at least two minutes for the modem to cycle through the self-tests. If it's already on, turn it off and on again. (If you have a battery pack to keep it from turning off, remove that for a few seconds, and then reinsert it.)

5. Turn on the hub or switch. Wait at least two minutes for the hardware to perform the self-tests.

6. Turn on the PC that is connected directly to the hub or switch.

7. Open the Network and Sharing Center. You'll see something similar to what's shown in Figure 4-1.

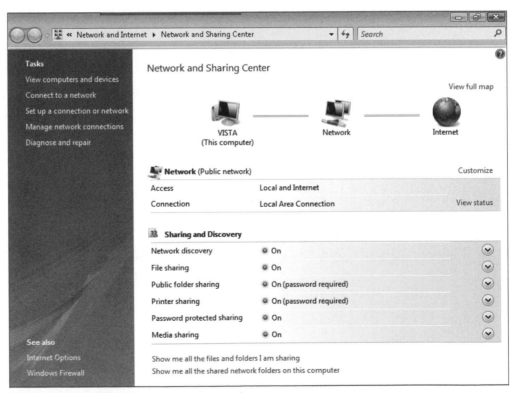

Figure 4-1 The network is connected properly.

ROUTERS

Before setting up your router, read all the instructions that came with it. You'll have to connect to the Internet to make it work, and you'll have to use Internet Explorer when configuring the router. Because setup differs from manufacturer to manufacturer, it's impossible to cover the exact steps here. However, generally you'll need to do the following:

1. Install the router software. The software is on a disc included with the router.

2. Connect the router to the cable modem and a PC. The router sits in the (virtual) middle of the router and the PC. The router's WAN port connects to the modem's Ethernet port; one of the router's Ethernet ports connects to the PC's Ethernet port.

3. Run the setup wizard provided by the router manufacturer. This process will help you log on to the router by using a Web browser and the router's IP address. To log on, you'll use the generic user name and password provided. Once logged on, change your user name and password, and continue the setup process.

4. When logged on and at the router's setup screen, configure how your ISP obtains an IP address. Almost always it's via Obtain An IP Address Automatically. If you aren't sure, call your ISP.

5. Save the changes and continue.

> **TIP** If you have a PC that does not have a port for plugging in an Ethernet cable (a.k.a. Ethernet card or NIC), you have several choices. You can purchase a NIC, open the case, and install the card; you can take the computer to a computer repair shop and let the technicians add the card; or you can purchase a USB-to-Ethernet converter. The latter is the easiest; all you have to do is insert the hardware into any open USB port.

UNDERSTAND THE BOOT ORDER FOR HARDWARE

If you are positive you've connected the hub, switch, router, cable modem, and Ethernet cables properly but you do not have access to the Internet or networked PCs, you need to recycle your hardware. You must do this in a specific order to work, as listed here. Before starting, turn off the PCs and unplug the hub, switch, or router.

POWER CYCLE THE CABLE MODEM

Unplug the power cord to the modem. If the modem has a battery backup that does not allow it to turn off, take out the battery as well. After a minute or so, plug the modem back in, and reinsert the battery if applicable. The cable modem will boot and run through myriad self-tests. After it's fully rebooted (usually between 30 seconds and 2 minutes after restoring power), continue.

POWER CYCLE THE ROUTER

Turn on the hub, switch, or router by plugging it back in and turning it on if necessary. Wait for another few minutes to make sure the router has completed rebooted.

TURN ON THE PCS

Restart the PCs that are connected to the router.

Personalize Your Network

By default, the name given to your new Windows Vista network is WORKGROUP. Additionally, the network may be configured initially as a public network, which is not nearly as secure as a private one. Finally, the network will not have network discovery turned on. You need to configure all this to make your network secure and to personalize it.

NAME THE NETWORK

For Windows XP, the default network name was MSHOME. If you upgraded a Windows XP computer to Windows Vista, the default name remained the same as it was before you upgraded, whether that was MSHOME or something else you created. If you purchase a new Windows Vista–based PC, though, it's automatically WORKGROUP.

It's best if all computers on your network use the same network name. If they don't, you'll have a hard time sharing data and hardware. You shouldn't leave the network name as WORKGROUP or MSHOME, though, because that's the default, and if at any time a hacker does try to access your network, you can bet these are the first names the hacker will try.

To change the name of your network and create something unique for you, follow these steps:

1. Click Start, right-click Computer, and click Properties.

2. Note the Workgroup name. As shown in Figure 4-2, it's WORGROUP. Click Change Settings to modify the name.

3. Click Continue, and in System Properties, also shown in Figure 4-2, click Change.

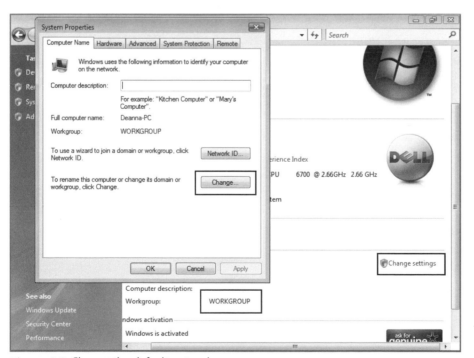

Figure 4-2 Change the default network name.

4. Type a new name for the network. Click OK, OK, and OK again.

5. Click Close.

6. Close any open programs, and restart the computer.

MAKE THE NETWORK PRIVATE

Networks come in one of three types: domain, public, and private. You won't have a domain if you've been following along here. Domains are reserved for organizational intranets, such as those found in large corporations. To have a domain, you need an Active Directory domain controller, which you likely don't have. That leaves two choices for your network, public and private.

A *public network* is a computer that is connected to a network and has a direct connection to the Internet. You'll find these types of networks in libraries, schools, and coffee shops. You do not have a public network.

A *private network* is a network used for personal access to the Internet and connects to trusted computers. This is the kind of network you have. Private networks are used for homes, home offices, small businesses, and similar locations. Private networks also include an Internet gateway device, such as a router, to protect the network from incoming traffic from the Internet.

To make sure you have a private network configured and not a public one, and to change it if necessary, follow these steps:

1. Click Start, right-click Network, and click Properties.

2. Verify that the network is private, as shown in Figure 4-3. If it is not, continue; if it is, skip to the next section.

3. Click Customize.

4. Choose Private.

5. Click Next and then Close.

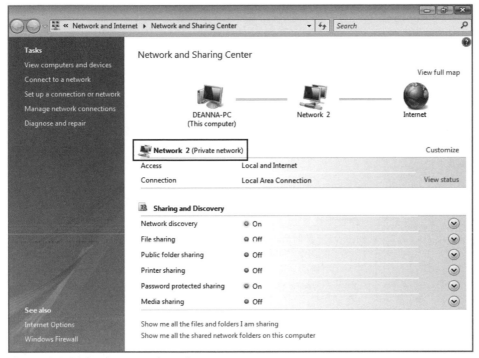

Figure 4-3 Make the network a private one.

TURN ON NETWORK DISCOVERY

By default, network sharing and discovery is turned off on your Windows Vista–based machine. This is to protect your PC from unauthorized access. You need to turn on network discovery so you can see other computers on the network and share files, folders, media, and printers.

It's important to note that just because the Network and Sharing Center shows a network is configured (as in Figure 4-1) and you are connected to the Internet, this does not mean the network is configured properly. You must turn on network discovery and establish what you want to share.

On the Windows Vista–based computer, follow these steps:

1. Click Start, click Control Panel, and then open Network and Internet.

2. Open the Network and Sharing Center.

3. As noted, network discovery is turned off by default. To turn it on, click the down arrow by Network Discovery, and click Turn On Network Discovery, as shown in Figure 4-4.

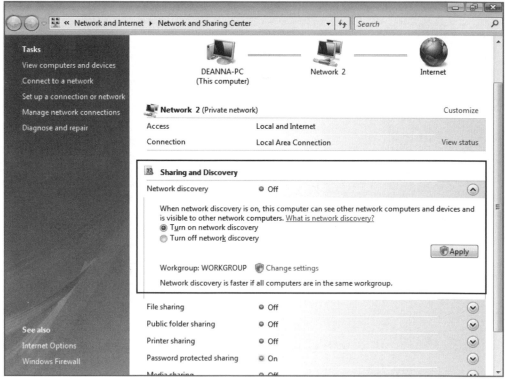

Figure 4-4 Turn on network discovery so you can view and access the second computer and its shared data.

4. Click Apply.

5. Click Continue to verify you want to turn on network discovery.

6. If prompted whether to turn on network discovery for all public networks, select No, Make The Network That I Am Connected To A Private Network.

You'll learn more about file, folder, and printer sharing in Chapter 6, including turning on file sharing, requiring passwords to connect, and more.

Add PCs

With the hub, switch, or router installed and configured and with a working cable modem or other Internet connection, you can now add PCs to your wired Ethernet network.

> **TIP** No matter what happens when you physically add the second Windows Vista–based PC—for instance, if you can connect to the Internet and therefore think the network automatically configured itself—you still need to work through the following steps. You must add the new PC to the network properly.

ADD AND TURN ON A WINDOWS VISTA–BASED PC

To add another Windows Vista–based PC, first connect the new PC to the hub, switch, or router by using an Ethernet cable. Once connected, you'll need to introduce the computer to the network. Although you can do this in lots of ways, here's one that never fails:

1. Click Start, right-click Computer, and click Properties.

2. Click Change Settings to modify the network name.

3. Type the name of the network. Click Next.

4. Click Close.

5. Click Start, click Network, and click Network And Sharing Center.

6. Verify network discovery is on. If it is not, turn it on.

To verify you've done this correctly, in Network double-click the Windows Vista–based PC. Type a user name and password that is valid on the Windows Vista–based PC. You'll be able to see the shared folders on the PC. Figure 4-5 shows the Windows Vista shared files, folders, and hardware.

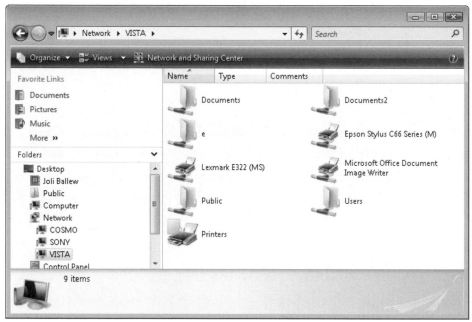

Figure 4-5 Log on to a network computer to verify everything is working properly.

ADD WINDOWS XP–BASED PCS

The first step to adding a Windows XP–based PC, or any other for that matter, is to connect the PC to the hub, switch, or router. Once connected, especially if a broadband modem is involved, you may have automatic access to the Internet through it. Don't mistake this for network connectivity, though. When you look further, you'll quickly find the only PC you can see on the network is the Windows XP–based PC.

You'll need to work through the Network Setup Wizard to fully connect to the network. (No matter what type of access you have, work through the following steps.)

To add a Windows XP–based PC to an existing wired Ethernet network, follow these steps:

1. Click Start, and click My Network Places.

2. In Network Tasks, select Set Up A Home Or Small Office Network. Click Next to begin.

3. Read the Before You Continue list, and make sure you've installed any network cards, modems, and cables; make sure you've turned on the other computers, printers, and external modems on the network; and make sure there's a connection to the Internet. Click Next.

4. Select the statement that best describes the computer you're adding. Most likely, you'll select This Computer Connects To The Internet Through A Residential Gateway Or Through Another Computer On My Network. (A *residential gateway* is a device that provides broadband connectivity to the PCs on your network. The connection can be cable, DSL, satellite, or wireless.) Select this if you use a cable modem with a hub, switch, or router or if you access the Internet through a shared dial-up connection from the Windows Vista–based PC. Click Next.

5. Type a computer name and description. The computer name must be unique on the network. Make sure to create a name, or use the default name, that is not or will not be repeated on the network. Click Next.

6. Type the name of your network, and click Next. Figure 4-6 shows an example. If you do not know the name of your network, on the Windows Vista–based PC follow these steps:

   a. Click Start, and right-click Computer.

   b. Select Properties.

   c. Look for the workgroup name.

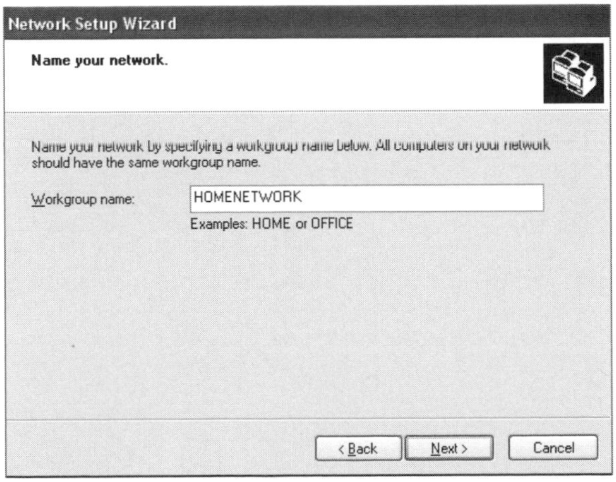

Figure 4-6
Configure the network on Windows XP.

7. Select Turn On File And Print Sharing. Click Next.

8. Click Next again.

9. When setup completes, select Just Finish The wizard; I Don't Need To Run The Wizard On Other Computers. Click Next.

10. Click Finish, and then click Yes to restart the computer.

To verify the network is configured correctly, follow these steps:

1. On the Windows XP–based PC, click Start, click My Network Places, and click View Network Computers.

2. Double-click any PC on the network, and log on if prompted by using a user name and password that works on that PC.

TIP Adding PCs running Windows ME or Windows 2000 is similar to what's detailed here. For these PCs, click Start, click Help And Support, and search for *network*. Follow the wizards provided.

ADD A MAC

If you have a Mac you want to add to your network, connect it via Ethernet as detailed previously. Once connected, you'll need to configure both the Mac and the PC for access. Follow these steps:

1. On the Mac, verify TCP/IP is configured properly, and write down the Mac's TCP/IP address.

2. On the Mac, turn on Personal File Sharing and Windows Sharing.

3. On the network PCs, do the following:

    a. For Windows Vista, log on with the proper credentials in Network.

    b. For Windows XP, create a new network place by using the Mac's IP address.

CONFIGURE THE MAC FOR SHARING AND PC ACCESS

To allow access from any PC on your network to the Mac, follow these steps:

1. From the Dock, open System Preferences.

2. Select Network.

3. For Location, select Automatic. Click OK. If you'd like, you can create a new location with the name of your network, but this is not required.

4. For Show, select Built-In Ethernet.

5. On the TCP/IP tab, verify Configure IPv4 is set to Using DHCP. Write down the TCP/IP address. It will be something along the lines of 192.168.1.*xxx*.

6. On the AppleTalk tab, verify Make AppleTalk Active is selected.

7. On the Ethernet tab, verify Configure is set to Automatically.

8. Click Apply Now.

9. Click Show All.

10. For System, select Sharing.

11. In Services, verify Windows Sharing is on.

12. In Services, verify Personal File Sharing is on.

13. In Firewall, verify the firewall is off.

14. Wait a few minutes before continuing so that the Mac has time to introduce itself to the network.

ACCESS THE MAC'S SHARED FILES FROM THE PC

You can access the Mac's shared files from any PC, but the setup differs for each operating system. Here is an explanation for connecting a Windows Vista–based PC and a Windows XP–based PC.

On the Windows Vista–based PC, follow these steps:

1. Click Start, click Network, and double-click the Mac computer.

2. Type a user name and password configured for the Mac.

On the Windows XP–based PC, follow these steps:

1. Click Start, and click My Network Places.

2. For Network Tasks, select Add A Network Place. Click Next.

3. Select Choose Another Network Location, and click Next.

4. For Internet or Network Address, type two backward slashes (\\), type the TCP/IP address you wrote down in step 5 in the previous section, type another backward slash (\), and type a user name. Make sure to get the syntax correct; Figure 4-7 shows an example.

5. Type a name for the network place. Mac Computer might work.

6. Click Finish.

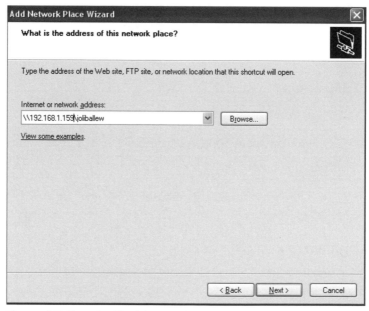

Figure 4-7 Type the IP address and user name.

ACCESS THE PC'S SHARED FILES FROM THE MAC

Back at the Mac, you must turn on direct access to the network. By default, you won't have access. To turn on network access, follow these steps:

1. Open the Finder, and select Mac HD.

2. Click Applications, then click Utilities, and finally click Directory Access.

3. Click the lock to make changes, and type a user name and password.

4. Click SMB/CIFS and then Configure. This is the choice for a network that connects to the Internet via broadband. If this option doesn't work, you'll have to experiment to find the choice right for you.

5. In Workgroup, select your workgroup name. Click OK.

6. Click Apply.

7. Click the lock to prevent changes, and close the Directory Access window.

To verify you can access files on the networked PCs, follow these steps:

1. In the Finder, select Network.

2. Click the network name.

3. Double-click the computer you want to access.

4. Type the workgroup name and a user name and password for that computer.

5. If you'd like, select Remember This Password In My Keychain. Click OK. (Keychain is a program that keeps passwords for you and is available on Apple computers.)

6. Select a share to access.

Unlike a PC, the shared folder won't open in the same window you used to authenticate. You'll find icons to the shared folders on the Desktop.

Chapter Summary

In this chapter, you learned how to set up an Ethernet network and add Windows Vista–based PCs, Windows XP–based PCs, and others. You learned a little about network discovery and sharing too. Skip to Chapter 6 for more information on sharing data on your network.

CHAPTER 5

The Wireless Network

- **Understand wireless network requirements**
- **Connect the hardware**
- **Configure the wireless router**
- **Understand the hardware's boot order**
- **Turn on the network**
- **Add PCs or a Mac**

A WIRELESS NETWORK is a must if you want to use your laptop computer to access the Internet or other home computers without being tethered to a cable; for instance, if you want to work and play outside with your laptop, you'll want a wireless network. Wireless networks also reduce the number of wires and cables you need and work well to reduce the clutter under and around your desk and TV. In general, wireless networks are more expensive and slower than Ethernet, but this likely won't pose a problem. Most new laptops ship with the required wireless hardware, and unless you're gaming across the network, you probably won't even notice a speed difference. Wireless transmissions can be affected by interference from devices, walls, and metal

...If you want to work and play outside with your laptop, you'll want a wireless network.

objects, but the ability to roam with your laptop and stream media throughout your home is often worth the trade-off. If you're still interested in setting up a wireless network, read on!

Get Started with Wireless Networking

This chapter is all about getting started with wireless networking, including understanding basic technologies, connecting the hardware, and configuring the router. Once you've set up the wireless router, you'll learn how to create a network and connect computers to it.

The first step you'll need to take if you're setting up a new wireless network is to decide on a technology. Wireless networks send data through radio waves, and there are currently three standards: 802.11b, 802.11g, and 802.11a. If you're out shopping for wireless hardware, make sure you look around for the newest, fastest, and most compatible hardware.

The 802.11g standard is the latest technology and transfers data at a rate of 54 Mbps. Newer 802.11g routers can transfer as fast as 108 Mbps. An 802.11a network transfers data at 54 Mbps. The 802.11b standard transfers data at a maximum rate of only 11 Mbps, so it's a bit slower than the a and g versions. The 802.11b standard has other issues too.

NOTE The 802.11n standard is the third-generation Wi-Fi standard for home networking but has yet to be officially ratified by the industry. This new standard will support speeds comparable to Fast Ethernet.

Because wireless networks send data by using radio waves, devices in a home can interfere with wireless signals and cause connections to become unreliable or cause transfer speeds to slow. Electronic devices such as cordless phones and microwave ovens can certainly cause problems. If you plan to send a lot of data across the network and you need it quickly such as with media or games, 802.11b wireless networks are not recommended because of slow speeds. The 802.11a standard is a good option because it is faster than 802.11b and operates on a separate frequency. This lessens the chance you'll experience interference. The 802.11g standard is suitable as well, but it may suffer the same interference problems you'll see with an 802.11b network.

Wireless network adapters and routers support three standards. As you might guess, 802.11b hardware is the least expensive. The a and g versions are more expensive, with 802.11g being the most costly, because 802.11g technologies are faster and offer a greater signal range than the others. When deciding on a technology, you'll have to weigh performance against price. You may also need to take into account hardware you already own, such as wireless network adapters already installed on computers, so you can purchase compatible products.

Connect the Hardware

The hardware you need for your wireless home network includes one wireless router (also called an *access point*) and a wireless network adapter for each computer on your network. As noted in the previous section, the technology you decide to go with, whether it's 802.11a, b, or g, might partially depend on what hardware you already own. You may even decide to create a network of mixed, compatible technologies. You'll also need a broadband connection (with a modem) to access the Internet.

Before you start connecting hardware, open everything you've purchased, and read the directions. Wireless routers come with instructions and an installation CD and the ability to create and modify your own personal wireless network settings. If you've purchased wireless network adapters, those items have installation CDs and instructions as well.

Although the Windows Vista operating system comes with the option to set up a wireless router or access point in the Network and Sharing Center, because routers differ, as do installation and configuration, it's often best to try installing them by using the CD that comes with the hardware first. If the manufacturer's CD and installation instructions fail and you can't get troubleshooting information from the manufacturer's Web site or tech support center, you can always then turn to the Network and Sharing Center.

CONNECT A CABLE, DSL, OR SATELLITE MODEM

You'll need an external modem (cable, DSL, or satellite) installed prior to setting up your wireless network. If you are not sure whether it's connected properly or whether you need to reinstall it, this section shows you how. For the most part, this won't be necessary because if you already use a modem to access the Internet, it'll already be set up and configured.

To set up a broadband modem, follow these steps:

1. Connect the modem to the PC with Windows Vista. You can make the connection by using a USB or Ethernet port. For security reasons, connecting with Ethernet is the better choice.

2. Connect the modem to the cable outlet in the wall, and verify it's connected to a power outlet. Turn on the modem. Insert the CD that came with your modem, and follow the installation instructions.

3. Verify the proper lights are blinking or lit on the modem before continuing.

INSTALL A WIRELESS ROUTER

Wireless routers come with an installation CD. Most of the time, you'll need to install that software first, while also connected to the Internet with a previous option. An installation wizard will walk you through the installation process, which is generally a driver, tutorials, and any other setup information you'll need to create your network. When installation completes, you'll be prompted to connect components, plug in the router, and possibly even reboot all components in a specific order to turn on the wireless network.

CONFIGURE BASIC SETTINGS

During setup, most of the basic settings will be configured for you, or you'll be asked to supply fundamental information. One of the basic settings options requires you to verify that your Internet connection does or does not require a login name and password. Other basic settings include a requirement for the Internet IP and DNS addresses to be obtained automatically, which will be set up for you, and whether you want to use additional third-party security services. Figure 5-1 shows a sample installation screen.

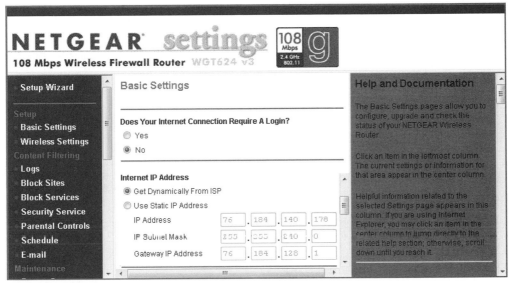

Figure 5-1 During installation, most of the basic settings will usually be configured automatically.

CONFIGURE WIRELESS SETTINGS

During setup, you'll also have to perform several tasks, including creating a wireless network name, technically called a *security set identifier* (SSID), creating a passphrase or password, and setting up security settings for the router and wireless computers, among other tasks. The setup CD should include information to help you make these decisions. However, on the slim chance there isn't any information about the decisions you'll be required to make, here are a few terms you should be familiar with:

SSID The name you'll create and use for the wireless network.

Region Your country or region.

Channel The operating frequency to be used. Usually you'll change this only if interference problems occur.

Mode The desired wireless mode:

    g and b Both 802.11g and 802.11b can be used.

    g only All equipment has to be g only.

    b only All equipment has to be b only.

    Auto The highest setting available from your router.

Encryption The security used to protect your network:

None No data encryption.

WEP Wired Equivalent Privacy, 64-bit or 128-bit. The 64-bit WEP option uses 10 hexadecimal digits (0–9 and A–F) for a password. The 128-bit option uses 26 hexadecimal digits.

Security Encryption (WPA-PSK, WPA2-PSK, WPA-PSK+WPA2-PSK) Wi-Fi Protected Access with Pre-Shared Key. The passphrase is 8 to 63 characters in length.

For the most part, installation will guide you through selecting and configuring the right settings for you. Although this may seem complicated, it isn't. It's just naming your network, selecting a mode, and creating a password to protect your network!

SET UP THE PHYSICAL CONNECTIONS

The physical connections initially include connecting the wireless router; a cable, satellite, or broadband modem; and a PC. The modem should already be installed and configured, though, as should the PC. The only element to add is the wireless router. Before continuing, make sure you place the router near the center of the area where all your PCs will operate, such as in the middle of your home. Make sure it's elevated; away from potential sources of interference, such as other PCs, microwave ovens, and cordless phones; and that the antenna is in the upright position. You want to position the wireless router in the middle of all your PCs so they each have access, so spend a few minutes deciding where would be the best place for it.

To add the wireless router, follow these steps:

1. Verify the cable modem is connected to a power outlet and the cable coming from the cable outlet in the wall.

2. Connect an Ethernet cable from the Ethernet out jack on the modem to the WAN port on the wireless router.

3. Connect an Ethernet cable from the Windows Vista–based PC to the wireless router.

4. Test connectivity by connecting to the Internet.

UNDERSTAND THE BOOT ORDER FOR HARDWARE

If you are positive you've connected the wireless router, modem, and Ethernet cables properly but you do not have access to the Internet, you may need to recycle your hardware. You must do this in a specific order to work, as listed here. Before starting, turn off the PCs, and unplug the wireless router.

POWER CYCLE THE CABLE MODEM

Unplug the power cord to the modem. If the modem has a battery backup that does not allow it to turn off, take out the battery as well. After a minute or so, plug the modem back in, and reinsert the battery if applicable. The cable modem will boot and run through myriad self-tests. After it's fully rebooted (usually between 30 seconds and 2 minutes after restoring power), continue.

POWER CYCLE THE ROUTER

Turn on the wireless router by plugging it back in and turning it on if necessary. Wait for another few minutes to make sure the router has completely rebooted.

TURN ON THE PCS

Restart the PC that is connected to the router.

VERIFY NETWORK DISCOVERY IS ON

Network discovery should be turned on for all your Windows Vista–based PCs. To verify this is so, on the Windows Vista–based computer follow these steps:

1. Click Start, click Control Panel, and then open Network.

2. Open the Network and Sharing Center.

3. If network discovery is turned off, turn it on. Click the down arrow next to Network Discovery, and click Turn On Network Discovery.

4. Click Apply.

5. Click Continue to verify you want to turn on network discovery.

6. If prompted whether to turn on network discovery for all public networks, select No, Make The Network That I Am Connected To A Private Network.

You'll learn more about file, folder, and printer sharing in Chapter 6, including turning on file sharing, requiring passwords to connect, and more.

Add a Windows Vista–Based PC

To add a second Windows Vista–based PC to the new wireless network, turn on the PC. It should have a wireless card installed or a wireless USB adapter. Once the PC is turned on, it should automatically see the new wireless network.

To add a second Windows Vista–based PC, follow these steps:

1. Turn on the PC, and insert or install, if necessary, the wireless card or wireless adapter.

2. Position the PC near the wireless router.

3. Position the pointer over the Network icon in the Notification area of the taskbar. The pop-up will indicate a wireless network is in range. See Figure 5-2. (Alternately, click Start, Network, and in the Network window select This Computer Is Not Connected To A Network. Click To Connect. Select Connect To A Network from the drop-down choices.)

4. Select the wireless network to connect to from the list. See Figure 5-3. Once selected, click Connect.

5. Type the security key or passphrase. The key or passphrase is case-sensitive. Click Connect. See Figure 5-4.

Figure 5-2 Rest your pointer on the Network icon in the Notification area to access available wireless networks.

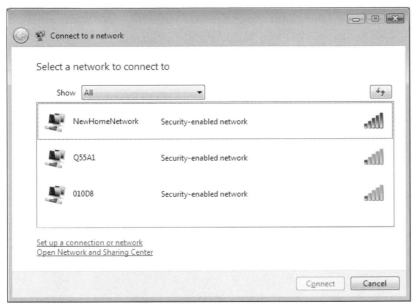

Figure 5-3 Select the appropriate wireless network.

Figure 5-4 Type the security key or passphrase to connect.

6. If desired, select Save This Network and Start This Connection Automatically. Click Close.

7. In the Set Network Location window, select the type of network to which you are connecting. In other words, if it's a home network, select Home. Other choices include Work and Public Location. Click Continue to verify you want to connect.

8. Click Close.

To access a network share, in the Network window, double-click any computer on the network, and when prompted, type an administrator name and password.

ADD WINDOWS XP–BASED PCS

To add a Windows XP–based PC to an existing wireless Ethernet network, follow these steps:

1. Turn on the PC, and insert or install, if necessary, the wireless card or wireless adapter.

2. Position the PC near the wireless router.

3. Click Start, Connect To, and select Wireless Network Connection.

4. If you see the warning shown in Figure 5-5, you installed a wireless management utility with your wireless network card or adapter. To turn off this secondary software and use the Windows XP wireless management software, locate the secondary wireless software, generally located in the Notification area of the taskbar, right-click the utility, and select Enable Wireless Zero Configuration (WZC). Then, click Refresh Network List in the Tasks pane, also shown in Figure 5-5. If you need more information, refer to Microsoft KB article 871122.

5. Select your network from the list, and click Connect. See Figure 5-6.

6. Type the network key two times. Click Connect. Once connected, you'll see the screen shown in Figure 5-7.

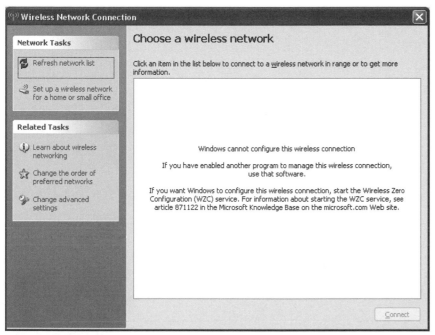

Figure 5-5 If you see this warning, set up the Wireless Zero Configuration utility.

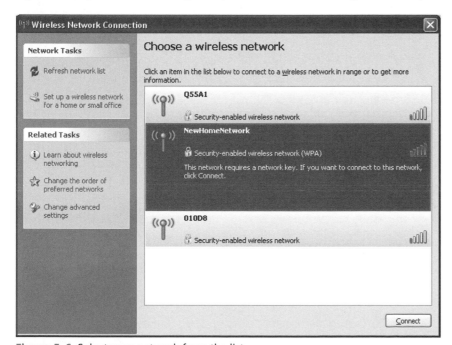

Figure 5-6 Select your network from the list.

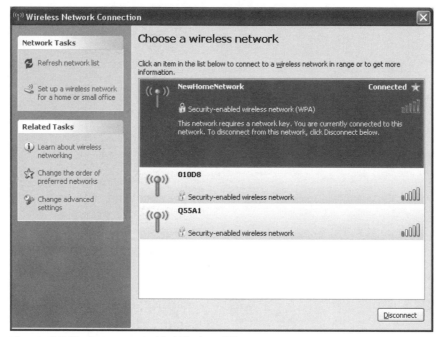

Figure 5-7 You're connected in Windows XP.

> **TIP** Adding PCs running Windows ME or Windows 2000 is similar to what's detailed here. For these PCs, click Start, click Help And Support, and search for *network*. Follow the wizards provided.

ADD A MAC

If you have a Mac you want to add to your network, position it close to the wireless router, and turn it on. Then follow these steps:

1. Using the Dock, select System Preferences.

2. Open Network.

3. In AirPort, select Configure.

4. In the TCP/IP Configure section, click Using DHCP Server.

5. Set the configuration to AirPort, and click the AirPort tab.

6. For the Preferred Network entry, click the down arrow to view the available wireless networks.

7. Select your network.

8. Close the window, and save the settings.

Once the Mac is connected, refer to Chapter 4 regarding how to share and access files between PCs and the Mac.

Chapter Summary

In this chapter, you learned how to set up a wireless network and add Windows Vista-based PCs, Windows XP–based PCs, and others. You learned about types of wireless networks, the hardware required to create one, and the boot order for components.

CHAPTER 6

The Network and Sharing Center

- **Review network discovery and network locations**
- **Share files and folders**
- **Configure Public folder sharing**
- **Share a printer**
- **Share media**
- **View and access all computers and devices**
- **View and access shared files and folders**

THE LAST FEW tasks in setting up a network are configuring the options in the Network and Sharing Center and then accessing the shared data and devices. In this chapter, you'll first learn how to share files, folders, media, and printers on your PC with the Windows Vista operating system. After that, you'll learn how to view and access the networked computers and the shared data and devices.

Sharing goes both ways, though. In this chapter, you'll configure sharing on the Windows Vista–based PCs, but you'll also have to share data from the PCs on your network that are not running Windows Vista.

In this chapter, you'll configure sharing on the Windows Vista–based PCs, but you'll also have to share data from the PCs on your network that are not running Windows Vista.

Although a number of sharing scenarios exist, for now I'll focus on using the public folders in Windows Vista (Public Documents, Public Pictures, and so on) and the shared folders in Windows XP (Shared Documents, Shared Pictures, and so on) for sharing data between the networked PCs. In Chapter 8, I'll go into more depth, including how to create your own shared folders and how to assign permissions.

> **TIP** It's best to work through the sections in this chapter from beginning to end.

Set Up Your Network Locations

When setting up your network locations, Windows Vista prompts you regarding what type of network it is. You have two choices: Public and Private.

Private Choose Private when you know and trust the people and devices on the network. Network discovery will be turned on by default. This way, you can see others, and they can see you. This is necessary to participate in a network.

Public Choose this location when connecting to a network at an airport, coffeehouse, club, or bar. This setting keeps your computer out of sight of others logged on to the same network. Firewall settings are configured at a higher security level to help keep malicious software off your computer too. If the settings block a program or application you want to use, you can always unblock the program if you need to do so.

To view or change your network location, open the Network and Sharing Center, and in Network, click Customize. In the Set Network Location window, shown in Figure 6-1, select the network type, and then click Next, Continue, and Close.

Figure 6-1 Use Set Network Location to change the network settings.

Configure Network Discovery

You learned in Chapters 3, 4, and 5 how to turn on network discovery, and I covered the features extensively. To review briefly, network discovery has two discovery states: on and off. When network discovery is on, your computer can see other network computers and devices, and other network computers and devices can see you. For a home network, you'll need to have this on. When network discovery is off, you cannot see other network computers, and they cannot see you.

When network discovery is on, you are able to select a type of network location. You have to select a network location to connect to a network. Based on the selection you make, whether it's a public or private network, Windows Vista tweaks the network discovery state and opens the appropriate Windows Firewall ports for you, as noted in the previous section. This allows you to go about the business of connecting to a network that's in range, even in a coffee shop, without having to worry about others seeing your PC or having the access necessary in a home or work setting.

Share Files

In the Network and Sharing Center, just under Network Discovery, is the File Sharing option. You can turn file sharing on or off. If you want to share files with others, it will need to be on.

To turn on file sharing, follow these steps:

1. Open the Network and Sharing Center.

2. Click the arrow under Sharing And Discovery next to File Sharing, as shown in Figure 6-2.

3. Select Turn On File Sharing.

4. Click Apply.

5. Click Continue.

Once file sharing is on, you can access Control Panel's power options from the Sharing And Discovery section. Again, click the arrow next to File Sharing. You will need to change the power options if you often put your computer to sleep. If your PC goes to sleep, others on the network will not be able to access your shared files or printers. Figure 6-2 shows the Power Options link and that file sharing is on.

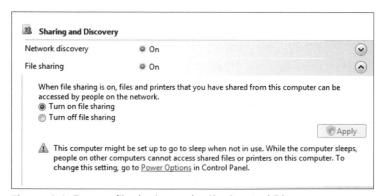

Figure 6-2 Turn on file sharing under Sharing And Discovery.

Share the Public Folder

Public folder sharing lets people on the network access files that are in the Public folder. The Public folder is a default folder automatically created for every user who has a user account on the computer.

Anyone who has a user account and a password can access what's in the Public folders, if you allow it. You have two choices for the Public folder; you can allow everyone who has a user name and password to access what's in it, or you can allow no one. You can also decide whether you want people to only access and read the items in the Public folder or whether they can make changes to them too.

To see the options for enabling Public folder sharing, follow these steps:

1. Open the Network and Sharing Center.

2. Click the arrow in Sharing And Discovery next to Public Folder Sharing.

3. Select one option from the following:

    - Turn On Sharing So Anyone With Network Access Can Open Files

    - Turn On Sharing So Anyone With Network Access Can Open, Change, And Create Files

    - Turn Off Sharing (People Logged On To This Computer Can Still Access This Folder)

4. Click Apply. Click Continue.

You have many options for locating the Public folder on your computer:

- Click Start, and in the Start Search box, type **Public**. In the results for Files, select the Public folder.

- Click Start and then Network. Click Public in the Folders pane.

- Right-click Start, click Explore All Users, and click Public in the Folders pane.

You can create subfolders in the Public folder to further personalize the folder and allow access to additional data stored on your hard drive. In Figure 6-3, you can see the default folders (selected), additional folders I've created, and one shortcut.

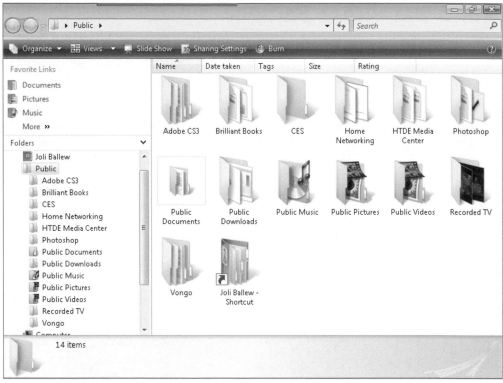

Figure 6-3 Access Public folders, and create your own subfolders and shortcuts.

Share Printers

Next in line under Sharing And Discovery is Printer Sharing. You'll turn on printer sharing the same way you turned on other sharing options. Click the arrow to the right of Printer Sharing, and select Turn On Printer Sharing.

You can access shared printers on Windows Vista from Control Panel's Printer option. In the Printers window, you'll see all the printers you have access to on the network, as well as shared printers. Shared printers have an icon by them that looks like two people standing together, as shown in Figure 6-4.

To see the default sharing properties, right-click any shared printer, and click Properties. Click Change Sharing Options, and you'll see the dialog box shown in Figure 6-5. You'll learn more about printer sharing in Chapter 9.

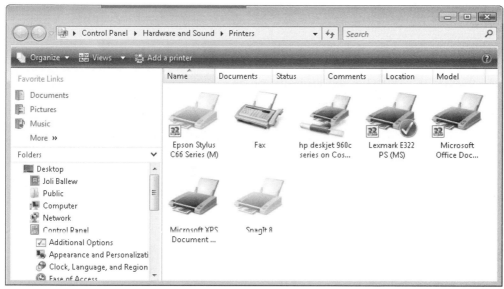

Figure 6-4 Shared printers have a special icon beside them.

Figure 6-5 You can set printer sharing options by clicking Properties and clicking Change Sharing Options.

Use Password Protection

Another option in the Network and Sharing Center is Password Protected Sharing. It has two settings, on and off. When password-protected sharing is on, people on your network who have a user account and a password on this computer can access shared files, share printers on this computer, and access the Public folder. If you want other people to be able to access these items, specifically those who do not have a user account and password on this computer, you'll need to turn the Password Protected Sharing option off.

Share Media

When media sharing is turned on, people and devices on your network can access shared music, pictures, and video stored on this computer. Additionally, the Windows Vista–based PC can find those types of shared files on network computers too.

To turn on media sharing, follow these steps:

1. Open the Network and Sharing Center.

2. Click the arrow in Sharing And Discovery next to Media Sharing. Click Change.

3. In the Media Sharing dialog box, shown in Figure 6-6, select Share My Media.

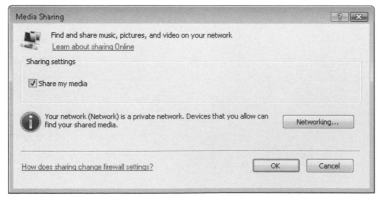

Figure 6-6 Share media such as pictures, music, and video.

4. Click OK and Continue.

5. Again, click the arrow in Sharing And Discovery next to Media Sharing. Click Change.

6. Select Other Users Of This PC, and click Allow.

7. To make changes to the default media sharing settings, click Customize.

8. Deselect Use Default Settings, and select only the media you want to share. You can choose from Music, Pictures, and Video.

9. Configure the Star Ratings settings.

10. Configure the Parental Ratings settings.

11. Figure 6-7 shows some sample settings. Click OK.

12. Click Settings to change the name of the shared media.

13. Click OK, and then click OK again.

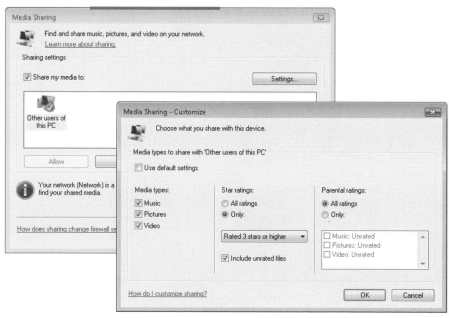

Figure 6-7 Configure shared media settings.

View Computers and Devices

With a network configured and sharing turned on, you should now be able to access shared files and folders, media, and other PCs from your Windows Vista–based PC as well as from other PCs on the network.

From the Windows Vista–based PC, click Start and then Network. Figure 6-8 shows an example of what you'll see. Here, three PCs—COSMO, SONY, and VISTA—are on the network, and VISTA is configured to share media.

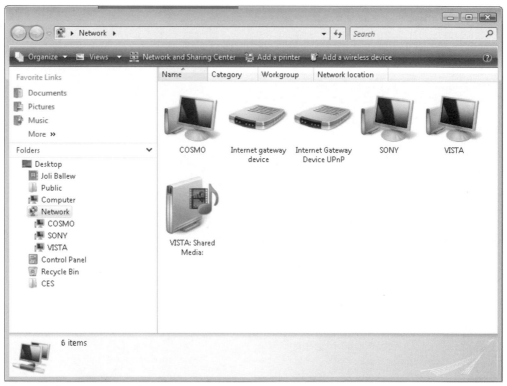

Figure 6-8 Locate network PCs.

To access any shared folders, printers, or other media on any other PC on the network, double-click the icon for that PC. Figure 6-9 shows what happens when double-clicking SONY, which is running Windows XP Professional. So, instead of seeing Public folders, you see SharedDocs. (Inside the SharedDocs folder is My Music, My Pictures, and My Video.)

Figure 6-9 These are the shared printers and documents on one network
Windows XP–based computer.

When browsing the network from the Windows XP–based PC, click Start and then
My Network Places. Select any shared public folder on the Windows Vista–based
PC. Figure 6-10 shows an example.

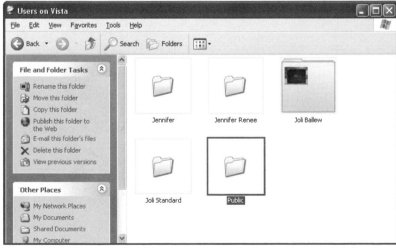

Figure 6-10 These are the shared documents and printers on a Windows
Vista–based PC viewed from a Windows XP–based PC.

Compare what's shown in Figure 6-10 to what was shown earlier in Figure 6-3. You can now view and access all shared folders in the Windows Vista Public folder from any PC on the network, although depending on your settings, it may require a password for access.

Chapter Summary

In this chapter, you learned how to complete the network setup process by using the Network and Sharing Center. You learned how to share files, Public folders, printers, and media, as well as how to access shared data after it has been set up.

PART III

Managing the Network

CHAPTER 7

Create User Accounts and Set Parental Controls

- **Understand how user accounts play a role on a single PC and a network PC**

- **Select appropriate account types for your users**

- **Create a user account**

- **Configure account properties**

- **Set parental controls on any account**

USER ACCOUNTS help you keep the data on your PC and your network safe. User accounts give people who have been given access to the computer and network the ability to keep their private data private, while also easily sharing data they regard as public.

User accounts are also created to personalize the computer for each user. Information saved in a user account tells the Windows Vista operating system what folders are a user's defaults and what each user has configured as their Desktop background, screen saver, monitor resolution, and other settings.

When each user has their own account, you can set restrictions and limitations so that each user has access to only the data they need and none of the other users' personal data.

For user accounts to work, though, each person who has access to a computer or the network must log on with their own user name and password. Users must log off when they are finished using the computer too. (A security hole is created when a user does not log off, leaving the PC and network available to others who should not have access.) Each time a user logs on with their user name and password, they have access to their own settings, folders, mail accounts, and more. User accounts are extremely important to keep a network safe and secure, and this chapter covers the topic in depth.

Understand User Accounts on the Single PC

Sometimes one networked PC is shared among multiple users. This is especially true of a computer you keep in the family or recreation room. Your children may access a shared computer for researching homework assignments, the cook of the house may access it to obtain recipes online, and the family planner may access it to create and maintain schedules for all family members. As with any networked PC, when one PC is shared among multiple users, each user should have their own account on the PC.

When each user has their own account, you can set restrictions and limitations so that each user has access to only the data they need and none of the other users' personal data. You can also set limitations for children regarding when they can access the computer and for how long. Finally, user accounts allow you, the administrator, to decide who can and cannot do potentially damaging acts, such as downloading and installing software or changing system-wide settings. Also, users can personalize their computer's view with backgrounds and screen savers, program settings, and similar options. When they log on using their user name and password, they'll see what they configured.

Understand User Accounts on the Networked PC

When each user on the network has a user account and password, you can control who has access to what, including users' personal data and media such as pictures, music, and video, as well as even whether users have access to data in public folders. You control who has access to what network data. You can also control a user's ability to install programs or change system-wide settings, which can be potentially harmful if incorrectly applied to a PC.

When each user has a user name and password, Windows Vista assigns specific rights and permissions to them by default. These rights and permissions include requiring administrator credentials to perform tasks such as accessing password-protected data, making changes to printer settings, installing or deleting software, adding or deleting data, and making changes to parental controls or other restricted settings. Also, users can personalize their view of their computer with backgrounds and screen savers, program settings, and similar options. That being said, it's extremely important to create user accounts for everyone you want to have PC or network access.

Understand Types of Accounts

Windows Vista offers three types of user accounts: administrator, standard, and guest. You have to be an administrator to create an account, so make sure you've logged on with your own administrator credentials before continuing. An administrator account is created during installation and setup, and it's likely you're logged on as an administrator now.

ADMINISTRATOR

An administrator account is the account you created when you set up Windows Vista. This account is the one you'll use to install programs, change security settings, install hardware and drivers, and access all the files on the computer. This is also the account you'll use when you want to create additional user accounts.

Because administrator accounts offer full access to the computer, it's best to use the administrator account only when necessary. You should create a standard account for yourself and all the other users who will have access to the computer. This way, if a rogue program, spyware, adware, or other malicious content tries to change a system-wide settings on your PC and you're logged on as a standard user, at least you'll have to type administrator credentials to allow it. This helps keep you and your PC safe.

STANDARD USER

A standard user account allows the user to do anything an administrator can, except for anything that will affect everyone who uses the computer. This includes but is not limited to installing hardware and software, deleting important operating system files, deleting a user's personal files, and changing security settings. Administrator credentials are required to make these changes.

GUEST

As you might guess, a guest account is for users who do not have a permanent account on your computer or network. This account allows users to access your computer to perform simple tasks such as writing a letter, sending and receiving Web-based e-mail, and printing to a local printer. By default, the guest account is turned off, and you should turn it on only when needed.

Create a User Account with a Password

The first user account you create should be a standard user account for yourself. Once you've created other user accounts and configured your PC, you can log on to that account when you access your computer, instead of logging on with your administrator credentials. To create additional accounts, log on with your administrator credentials.

CREATE A STANDARD USER ACCOUNT

To create a standard account for yourself, follow these steps:

1. Click Start, click Control Panel, and under User Accounts And Family Safety, select Add Or Remove User Accounts.

2. Click Continue.

3. Click Create A New Account.

4. Type the new account name, as shown in Figure 7-1, and select Standard User. Remember, this is your account, so create a name you like. I've created an account named Joli Standard so I can remember it's my standard account.

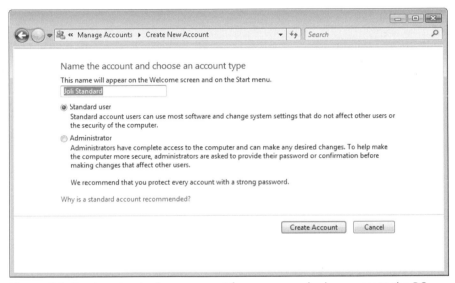

Figure 7-1 Create a standard user account for everyone who has access to the PC.

You'll create administrator accounts in the same manner. To turn on the guest account, click it in User Accounts, Manage Accounts, and then click Turn On.

CREATE A PASSWORD FOR THE NEW ACCOUNT

Continuing from the previous steps, add a password for the new account:

1. Click Create Account.

2. Click the new account to configure a password for it.

3. Click How To Create A Strong Password, and then read the information given.

4. Click Create A Password.

5. Type the new password, type the password again to confirm it, and type a password hint. Click Create Password, as shown in Figure 7-2.

Figure 7-2 Every user account needs a password.

TIP Each time you are finished using the computer, click Start, click the arrow circled in Figure 7-3 (shown later in the chapter), and click Log Off.

CREATE A PASSWORD RESET DISK

You should create a password reset disk only as a safety precaution. A password reset disk lets you reset your password if you ever forget it. Although this might not seem likely, it does happen. Unfortunately, if the floppy, CD, or DVD is found, anyone can use it to reset your password, so you should keep the disk in a safe place. Don't carry it with you in your laptop bag!

To create a password reset disk, follow these steps:

1. Click Start, Control Panel, User Accounts And Family Safety, and User Accounts.

2. In the Tasks pane, select Create A Password Reset Disk.

3. Click Next to start the wizard.

4. Select a disk drive to create the reset disk. Although you can use a floppy drive, chances are you don't have a floppy drive in your new Windows Vista–based PC. If this is the case, choose a drive offered. You can copy the information to a floppy, CD, or DVD later. Click Next.

5. Type your current user account password. Click Next.

6. Click Next and Finish.

> **TIP** You can also manage your network password in User Accounts. It's just below Create A Password Reset Disk in the Tasks pane. To back up these passwords, click Manage Your Network Passwords, and then click Back Up.

LOG ON TO YOUR NEW STANDARD ACCOUNT

A new account creates a pristine environment, ready to be personalized. To see what happens when you log on with your new account, follow these steps:

1. Click Start, click the arrow shown in Figure 7-3, and click Switch User.

2. In the Welcome Screen, select your new account.

3. Type your password, and click Enter.

You'll have to wait for Windows Vista to prepare your Desktop. Once logged on, the computer will react as a new computer would. The Welcome Center opens, and you have only the Recycle Bin on your Desktop. Windows Sidebar opens with the default gadgets. You can now personalize this account however you'd like and use it to log on each time you access the computer. If you try to access anyone's personal data, you'll be prompted to type their password for access.

Figure 7-3 Use the Start menu choices to log off or switch users.

To access the data stored on your administrator account, follow these steps:

1. Right-click Start, and select Explore All Users.

2. In the Folders pane, expand Local Disk.

3. Scroll down, and expand Users.

4. To open your administrator files, double-click your account, and when prompted, type your password.

You can now move or copy the files from your old account's folders to your new one, or you can repeat steps 1–4 each time you need access.

NOTE By default, the Fast User Switching option is on, which allows users to stay logged on with their programs running even when others need access. Thus, when you are finished with your computer, you can click either Switch User, which will leave you logged on and your open programs running, or Log Off, which closes everything and logs you off the computer completely. Either way, the Welcome Screen appears, and a password is required to log on to any password-protected user account, including your own.

Set Advanced Account Properties

Although the default account properties will likely suffice, you should be aware that you can assign some advanced properties. You are already aware of the importance of creating passwords, but of equal importance are some hidden security properties such as file encryption certificates and advanced profile properties. Although you might not want to change these settings, it does not hurt to know they exist and what they offer.

FILE ENCRYPTION

A file encryption certificate lets you encrypt your files for additional security. However, you must have an encryption certificate and an associated decryption key. You have to use the decryption key to access encrypted files. Many people store their encryption keys on a smart card.

By using the File Encryption Wizard, you can create an encryption certificate and key, back up the certificate and key, set the computer to use a smart card, and update previously encrypted files for the new certificate and key.

If this sounds like something you're interested in, the wizard is available by clicking Control Panel, User Accounts And Family Safety, User Accounts. Then select Manage Your File Encryption Certificates in the Tasks pane.

ADVANCED PROFILE PROPERTIES

User profiles store settings for a user's Desktop, screen saver, default folders, mail settings, and more. If you use your account to access more than one computer on the network, you can create a different profile for each computer you use. You can also set a roaming profile so that settings are the same on all the computers you use. By default, your profile is a local profile. You can change it to a roaming profile from the User Profiles dialog box shown in Figure 7-4, which you can access by clicking Control Panel, clicking User Accounts, and in the Tasks pane clicking Configure Advanced User Profile Properties.

Figure 7-4 User profiles store personalized settings for each user.

Set Parental Controls

Windows Vista offers a new way to help you control what your kids are doing when logged on to the computer with their standard accounts. You can do more with parental controls than just manage what your kids do, though. If you work in an office, for instance, you can set parental controls to define when your employees can log on to their computers and define whether they can play games. In addition, the new parental controls let you set limits for what hours any standard user can log on and what programs they can run. If a user tries to access something that's restricted because of rules you've set, the user can click the link in the notification box that appears and request permission from you to view or access it.

As you well know, though, in order for parental controls to work, everyone needs their own user account and password. If you leave the computer unattended and logged on with another account, your child can use that account to get around parental controls.

> **TIP** Children need standard accounts in order for parental controls to be applied. Parental controls cannot be applied to administrator accounts.

ACCESS PARENTAL CONTROLS

In Control Panel's User Accounts and Family Safety, select Parental Controls. You'll have to click Continue or log on with administrator credentials to access it. Select a standard user to which to apply parental controls. You'll see the Parental Controls options, as shown in Figure 7-5.

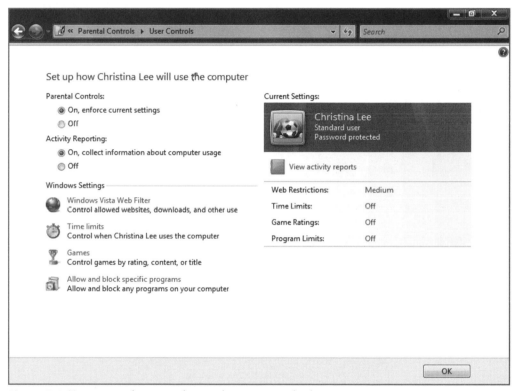

Figure 7-5 You can apply parental controls to any standard user account.

WEB RESTRICTIONS

Using the Windows Vista Web Filter shown in Windows Settings in Figure 7-5, you can control what Web sites your kids (or other users) visit, what they can download, and other similar Web uses. You can block *some* Web sites and content, allow *all* Web sites and content, allow access to only the Web sites that you add manually to the Allow list, or choose an automatic restriction level. Click Windows Vista Web Filter to see the options.

The automatic levels offered are quite inclusive. The settings include High, Medium, None, and Custom. Generally, a High restriction level will work; however, it is certainly possible to list five Web sites and allow your children access only to those five.

TIME LIMITS

You can set the hours you want certain users such as your children to have access to the computer. To configure blocked hours, drag the pointer over the hours to block. Blocked hours will turn blue. The hours in white are the hours the child can log on. See Figure 7-6.

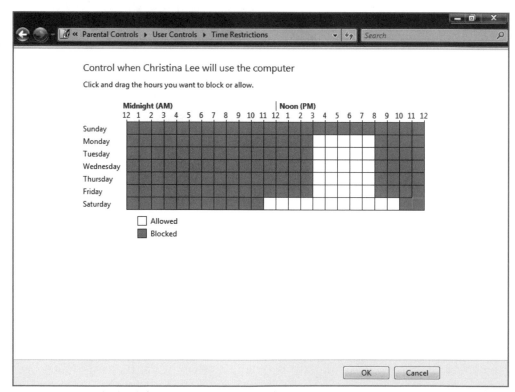

Figure 7-6 Time limits define when your child can log on.

GAMES

With Games settings, you can decide whether your children (or employees) can play games. If you choose Yes, you set game ratings and block or allow specific games. The best option is to block games with no rating and to then select the option that fits your child's age. You can block games by content too, including games (even those that meet other criteria) that contain references to alcohol, blood, gore, nudity, and other inappropriate content.

PROGRAMS

Finally, you can allow or block specific programs installed on your computer. If you choose to configure what programs your child can use, you'll need to place a check by the ones you allow. I allow access to photo programs for Christina Lee, but not much else.

View Parental Control Reports

Parental control reports spell out exactly what your child has done at the computer. When you first open the report, you'll see quite a bit of information. The information shown is categorized into several parts. In User Account Activity, you'll see the following:

Web Browsing A list of Web sites your child accessed and tried to access (including a list of Web sites that were blocked)

System A list of logon times and lengths

Applications A list of the applications run

Gaming A list of games played

Email Information regarding e-mail activity

Instant Messaging Information about your child's instant messaging activities

Media A list of songs, movies, and other media played

By default, the information for User Account Activity is selected and shown in a one-page report. However, you can also view the categories and subcategories separately. Selecting any of these subcategories in the left pane offers information regarding that particular subcategory.

To locate the parental control report, you'll first need to log on with an administrator account. Then follow these steps:

1. Click Start.

2. In the Start Search box, type **Parental Controls**.

3. Under Programs, click Parental Controls.

4. Select the user for which to view the parental control report.

5. Select View Activity Reports.

Chapter Summary

In this chapter, you learned all about user accounts, including how to create them. You learned that logging on with a standard account is much safer than an administrator account, and you learned how to create and turn on a guest account when needed. You also learned how to apply parental controls to your children's standard accounts as well as how to access and view activity reports.

CHAPTER 8

Configure and Manage Shared Folders

- **Create your own folders to share or share default folders**
- **Understand and apply default permissions**
- **Understand and apply advanced permissions**
- **Understand NTFS permissions**
- **Locate shared folders on network PCs**

IN CHAPTER 6, you learned a little about file and folder sharing, specifically data you deposit in the built-in Public folders. When you put data in a Public folder and allow access to it in the Network and Sharing Center, everyone who has permission to log on to the network or computer can access it—if you allow that.

In this chapter, I'll take sharing a little further. Here, you'll learn how to share default folders such as Documents and how to create your own folders to share. Once you've shared some folders, you'll learn how to configure default and advanced permissions as well as how to access those folders from other PCs on your network. By setting permissions on the folders you share, you stay in control of who has access to your data and what they can do with it once they access it.

Basic sharing is a right-click away, and default permissions are applied to your shared folder automatically.

Create Your Own Shared Folders

You can share folders that belong to you, whether they are default folders built in to the Windows Vista operating system or folders you create. Whatever you choose, the process is the same. Basic sharing is a right-click away, and default permissions are applied to your shared folder automatically.

SHARE A DEFAULT FOLDER

To share a folder that is your own—perhaps your Documents folder, Pictures folder, or Contacts folder—first locate the folder. You can locate most default user folders from the Start menu, from the Desktop, or from the network. Once you've located the folder to share, follow these steps:

1. Right-click the folder to share.

2. Select Share.

3. In the File Sharing dialog box, shown in Figure 8-1, note what it says about your sharing settings. Here, you can see that a user name and password are required for a user to access anything shared here. You can change this setting and other share settings in the Network and Sharing Center. If you want to make changes now, open the Network and Sharing Center, and make them before continuing. (Notice in Figure 8-1 that there are two accounts for Joli Ballew: one that's an administrator account and one that's a standard account. Both accounts have access currently.)

4. Click the down arrow just above the Name entries to see the users you can add or to add a new user, as shown in Figure 8-2. (If you choose to create a new user, User Accounts will open, and you'll need to create the user and return here once done.)

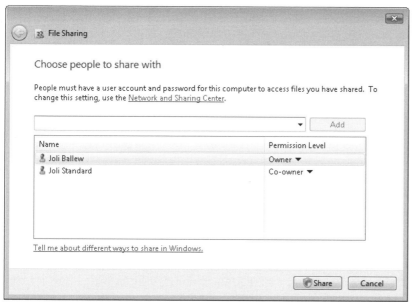

Figure 8-1 View your file sharing settings, and open the Network and Sharing Center to make changes.

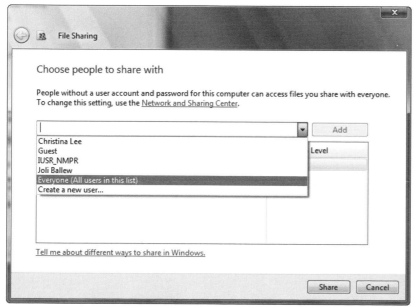

Figure 8-2 Create a standard user account for everyone who has access to the PC.

5. After selecting a user from the list, click Add. By default, the user is given Reader permissions. You can choose from Reader, Contributor, and Co-Owner. For now, click Reader. You'll learn more about these permissions and how to change them later, but for now click the down arrow under Permission Level to see the options.

6. Click Share. Click Continue.

7. Click Done. Notice that the folder now has a new icon beside it, indicating it's shared.

CREATE YOUR OWN SHARED FOLDER

You will probably want to create your own folder and folder structure for organizing data. Although the Documents folder may be good enough for personal data such as tax records, letters you've written, and a spreadsheet with your home budget, you will probably need folders that are more project- or task-specific to really stay organized.

Some folders I've created include folders named for book titles, personal Web sites, video projects, company information, client information, projects for online retailers, and proposals. You might need folders for accounting, advertising, budgets, sales contacts, hardware manufacturers, receipts, and more. Whatever the case, you'll eventually want to create a folder, put data into it, and then share it. Even if you're sharing it only so you can access it from another computer, you still need to share it.

To create your own folder and share it, follow these steps:

1. Locate where you'd like to store the new folder. The Desktop is certainly convenient, but consider creating the new folder in your Documents or Pictures folder, or creating an entirely new folder in your user folder, and filling it with appropriate subfolders. Creating the folder in Documents makes it easier to back up in the long run.

2. Right-click inside a folder or on the Desktop, whatever the case may be, and then click New, Folder.

3. Name the folder, and hit Enter.

4. Complete steps 1 to 7 in the previous section to share the folder and to apply default permissions.

Understand Default Permissions

When you create and share a folder, Windows Vista applies default permissions. The creator and owner of the folder has the highest-level permission, and people you add later have the lowest. You can choose from three permission levels: Reader, Contributor, and Co-Owner, as shown in Figure 8-3.

Reader Allows the person or group to view and read the files in a folder but not modify or delete the files. They can copy data in a file as well as the file itself.

Contributor Allows the person or group to view the files in the folder, add files, and change or delete files they add. They have Reader permissions to files and folders they did not create.

Co-Owner Allows the person or group to view, change, add, and delete all files in the shared folder, even ones they did not create.

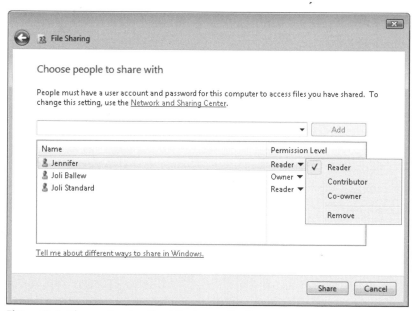

Figure 8-3 Choose Reader, Contributor, or Co-Owner.

When sharing a folder using default settings, consider the following:

- The owner is the person who creates the file. The owner has full control over the folder and the files in it as do co-owners.

- Sharing a folder shares everything inside it, including "nested" folders, called *subfolders*. You can make the folders in a shared folder private by using advanced sharing options, detailed later.

- Nested folders, even if made private, can be accessed and modified through the parent folder, but not if accessed directly through a network share. Thus, it's ultimately better to store private data outside any shared folders.

- You can hide any folder by typing a **$** symbol at the end of the share name during the sharing process. Users won't see it or know it exists. However, to access that folder yourself from another computer on the network, you'll need to click Start, type **Run** in the Start Search box, click Run in the Programs list, and then type the full path to the folder in the form of \\computername\hiddensharename.

SHOULD YOU SHARE WITH PUBLIC OR PERSONAL FOLDERS?

When you share data by using a Public folder (and turn on file sharing for the Public folder), anyone with a user account and password on your computer, as well as everyone on the network, can see all the files in that Public folder and its subfolders. You cannot let some people view some files in the Public folder and not view others, and you cannot let some people access the folder and not let other people. You can, however, decide whether people can change files or create new ones, but the rules apply to everyone who can access the data.

Sharing is different with personal folders. With this type of sharing, you get to decide everything, including who can make changes to what files, what kind of changes they can make, and who can access what. You can grant permissions to groups of people or to an individual (or individuals), while at the same time completely configuring what each can and cannot access. You can apply different permissions for everyone. You can't do that with Public folder sharing.

Use Public folder sharing if

- you want to share files from a single location for ease of management;

- you want to keep everything you share separate from your personal data; or

- it's okay with you to apply the same permissions for all users of your network and do not need to apply separate permissions for individuals.

Use personal folder sharing if

- you want to share data directly from your personal folders and don't want to move or copy the data to a Public folder;

- you need to apply separate permission for individuals regarding what they can do once they access your data, or if they can at all;

- you share large files you don't want to move or copy; or

- you frequently change what's shared.

CHANGE DEFAULT PERMISSIONS

If you gave a user the Reader permission and have now decided to change that permission, you'll need to access the sharing permissions for the folder to make the change.

To change a permission already applied to a user for a shared folder, follow these steps:

1. Right-click the folder you've already shared.

2. Click Change Sharing Permissions, as shown in Figure 8-4.

3. Click the arrow next to the permission to change, and select a new permission in the list.

4. Click Share, as shown in Figure 8-5. Note that you can e-mail the links to the shared data or copy the links onto the Clipboard and paste them into any program. By sharing the links with others, you can be sure they are aware of the shared data and where to find it.

5. Click Done.

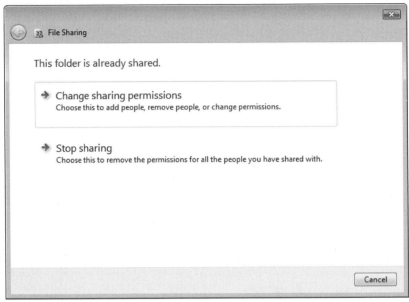

Figure 8-4 Once a folder is shared, click Change Sharing Permissions to alter the settings.

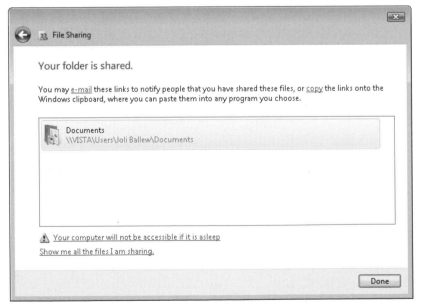

Figure 8-5 E-mail the link to others to make sure they know about the shared data and where to access it.

CAUTION Your user account prevents anyone who is using a standard account on your computer from seeing your files. It does not prevent other users with administrator accounts from seeing your files. If there are other administrator accounts on your computer besides your own, take this into consideration. If you must have multiple administrator accounts, protect your files with the Encrypting File System (EFS), briefly detailed later in this chapter.

APPLY ADVANCED SHARING

Advanced sharing options are not available by right-clicking the shared folder and clicking Share. Instead, you access them by right-clicking the shared folder, clicking Properties, and selecting the Sharing tab. Figure 8-6 shows an example. These are often called *power user* sharing options.

Figure 8-6 You achieve power user sharing through the Sharing tab.

To apply advanced sharing options, follow these steps:

1. Right-click the shared folder. Click Properties.

2. Click the Sharing tab.

3. Click Advanced Sharing.

4. Click Continue, and in the Advanced Sharing dialog box, select Share This Folder.

5. Choose how many users can have access at the same time. Choose from 1 to 10.

6. Click Permissions.

7. If desired, click Everyone, and click Remove. By removing everyone from the group, you can add one individual or one group at a time and configure them all separately. If you want to apply the permissions to everyone who has access to the computer, do not click Everyone, and instead skip to step 9.

8. Click Add to add a user to the list. Type the user name, and click Check Names. Continue in this manner until all users have been added. Click OK.

9. Select a user in the Group Or User Names list, shown in Figure 8-7.

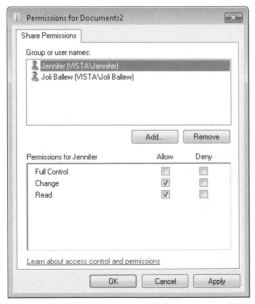

Figure 8-7 Select a user, and change permissions.

10. Select the Allow or Deny boxes as desired. Note that if you select Deny for Full Control, the other two Deny boxes are automatically selected. You have three choices:

   - **Full Control** Users have full control over the shared resource, including the ability to see and read data in it, change existing files and folders, create new files and folders, and run programs in the folder.

   - **Change** Users can add files to a folder, create folders, change data, and read files.

   - **Read** Users can only read files.

11. Click OK twice, and then click Close.

MAKE A SUBFOLDER PRIVATE (SORT OF)

The best way to keep private data private is to keep it out of a shared folder. So, first things first: If you have private data in a shared folder and it's possible to move it out of there, do that now, and then skip to the next section. If for some reason you must leave data you want to keep private in a shared folder, your best choice is to hide the folder. (There are other options, but this is the best option.)

To hide a folder in a shared folder so others cannot see it on the network or when logged on to the computer with their own user name and password, follow these steps:

1. Right-click the shared folder, and click Properties.

2. On the Sharing tab, click Advanced Sharing. Click Continue.

3. In the Advanced Sharing dialog box, select Share This Folder.

4. Type a share name, and put the **$** symbol after it, with no spaces between the file name and the symbol.

5. Click OK and Close.

Understand Security Permissions

The shared folders you've created can have one of three basic permissions: Reader, Contributor, and Co-Owner. For a basic home network, these permissions are suitable. But what if these just don't work for you? What if you want to let a user access a shared folder to read files and modify those files but not create new ones and not run any executable programs stored in the shared folder? That goes a bit beyond the default share permissions and must be configured by using security permissions.

Security permissions are referred to as *NTFS permissions*. NTFS (an acronym for *NT file system*) is a technology available in Windows Vista that lets you specify exactly what you want people to be able to do with shared data. You can configure something as complex as allowing three users to access and modify data while allowing two others to only access and read the data and while also allowing one user to only run programs and not even view the data—all on the same shared folder!

Be warned before continuing. Entire books have been written about applying these permissions. Thus, I won't go into detail regarding how to accomplish applying these permissions or what happens when you apply share permissions and NTFS permissions on the same folder. However, for the sake of completeness, I will provide an introduction, and if you'd like to take applying permissions a bit further, note that this is beyond the scope of this chapter and you'll need another book!

> **NOTE** You won't be able to apply NTFS permissions if your file system is not formatted with NTFS.

UNDERSTAND ADVANCED PERMISSION LEVELS

When setting advanced permissions, you have several to configure. For each, you can select Allow or Deny. Some options you can allow or deny include Modify, Read, and Write. This means you can let an individual read a file but not write to or modify it. When applying NTFS permissions, understand that Deny always wins over Allow. Choosing Deny for any category overrides any other permission granted, and that includes "inherited" permissions from parent folders.

Applying multiple permissions for multiple users is a little tricky, as you'd guess; it's often hard to determine just what a user can and can't do if you go overboard applying them. There's also the additional option Special Permissions, which really complicates things. Therefore, another word of caution: Apply advanced permissions only if you really must. Try to use the default permissions of Reader, Contributor, and Co-Owner first, and then move to advanced permissions only if those don't suit your needs. Table 8-1 lists the available NTFS permissions and a description of each.

Table 8-1
Permissions

PERMISSION LEVEL	DESCRIPTION
Full Control	Users can modify, execute, read, and write to files and folders.
Modify	Users can change files and folders but not create new ones.
List Folder Contents	Users can view file names and subfolder names within a folder.
Read & Execute	Users can see (read) files and folders and run programs.
Read	Users can see (read) the contents of a folder and open folders.
Write	Users can create new files and folders and can make changes to existing files and folders.
Special Permissions	Special permissions include permissions such as Take Ownership, Delete, and Synchronize.

NOTE I won't go into the Special Permissions option here. If you find that default and advanced permissions don't offer what you need, refer to the Help and Support files in Windows Vista for additional information.

APPLY SECURITY PERMISSIONS

If you want to apply NTFS permissions, right-click the shared folder, click Properties, and select the Security tab. Choose any user, and click Edit. Select a user from the Permissions dialog box or add a new user, and then apply the permissions as desired. Figure 8-8 shows what you might see when applying NTFS permissions.

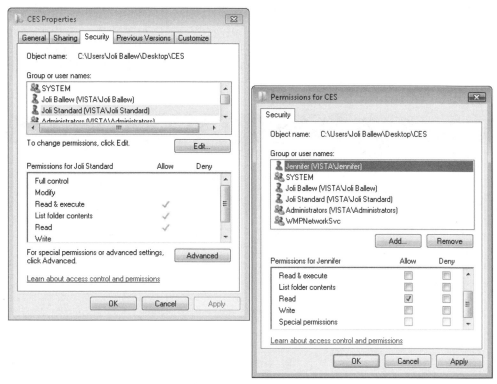

Figure 8-8 NTFS permissions are tricky to apply and manage.

Access Shared Folders from a Windows Vista–Based PC

Once folders are shared and permissions applied, you'll need to be able to access the shared folders and perhaps even create Desktop shortcuts to them. Although there are lots of ways to find and access shared folders, the best way is to click File and then click Network to select the computer that holds the shared folders and to access them.

To find and access a shared folder on a network, follow these steps:

  1. Click Start, and click Network.

  2. In the Network window, click the computer that holds the shared folder. Figure 8-9 shows an example of a Network window.

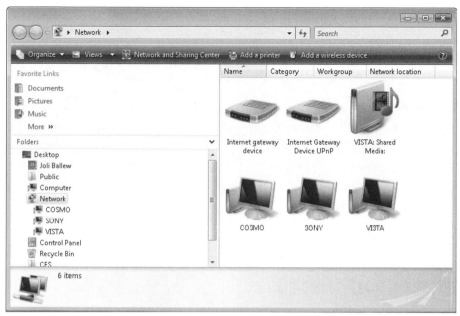

Figure 8-9 Double-click to browse the computer that holds the shared folder.

3. Browse through the available folders to locate the shared folder you want.

4. Type your user name and password if prompted. Click OK.

To create a shortcut on the Desktop to the shared folder, follow these steps:

1. Right-click the shared folder.

2. From the drop-down list, click Send To, and then click Desktop (Create Shortcut).

Access Shared Folders from a Windows XP–Based PC

To access shared folders on a Windows Vista–based PC from an Windows XP–based PC, click Start, click My Network Places, and select the shared folder from the list offered. If you do not see the shared folder you want to access, click Add A Network Place, and browse to it.

ENCRYPTING FILE SYSTEM

EFS technologies are available only in Windows Vista Business, Enterprise, and Ultimate. If you have Home Premium, you can skip this part!

EFS is a technology that stores data in an encrypted format. EFS doesn't require anything from you except that you turn it on. Files that are encrypted will be encrypted before saving them to the hard drive, and they will be decrypted when you need to work with them. To encrypt a folder or a file, right-click it, click Properties, and click the Advanced button. Select Encrypt Contents To Secure Data.

Chapter Summary

In this chapter, you learned how to create, configure, manage, and access shared folders. You learned about share permissions and NTFS permissions, and you learned how to apply them. I hope you've decided to share folders by using simple share permissions and to keep any personal data you do not want shared out of your shared folders. This is the best way to secure your personal files. Remember, though, an administrator can access all files on your computer, so make sure you're the only administrator if you want to really keep your stuff private!

CHAPTER 9

Turn On and Manage Printer Sharing

- **Share a connected printer**
- **Share a network printer**
- **Apply permissions**
- **Add a network printer**
- **Access a shared printer**

IF YOU HAVE a printer and a network, it's almost always best to share the printer with other network users. Sharing a printer reduces the need for multiple printers, allows others to print documents without accessing your PC, and lets you to manage the printer from your own Windows Vista–based computer.

Sharing a printer and managing it allows you to control whether users on other computers can render print jobs (in other words, print to the printer) and lets you add print drivers for PCs with alternative technologies. You can also decide whether to spool print documents, turn on advanced printing features, keep printed documents, configure

Sharing a printer is more than connecting it; it's an entire printer management system!

permissions to allow or deny users the ability to print, manage printers, manage documents, and do much more. Sharing a printer is more than connecting it; it's an entire printer management system!

Share a Printer with the Windows Vista Operating System

With a printer connected to a Windows Vista–based PC and turned on, you're ready to share it with others on the network. There aren't too many steps to basic sharing. You'll need to locate the printer in Windows Vista and then share it.

LOCATE THE PRINTER TO SHARE

First you'll need to locate the printer in Windows Vista. You can do this in several ways, but the easiest is to do the following:

1. Click Start, and in the Start Search box, type **Printers**.

2. From the results under Programs, click Printers.

Note that you can also open the Printers folder by clicking Start, Control Panel, Hardware And Sound, and Printers.

> **NOTE** If the shared printer is connected to a Windows XP–based PC, you'll need to perform similar tasks on that machine to share the printer. Refer to the sidebar "Share a Printer with the Windows XP Operating System" later in this chapter.

SHARE THE PRINTER

To share a printer with Windows Vista, follow these steps:

1. Right-click the printer to share.

2. Select Run As Administrator, and select Sharing.

3. Click Continue. The printer's Properties dialog box will open, and the Sharing tab will be selected automatically.

4. Select Share This Printer, shown in Figure 9-1.

5. Type a name for the printer in Share Name.

6. Select Render Print Jobs On Client Computers, also shown in Figure 9-1.

7. Read the information regarding printer sharing. In Figure 9-1 it states that when sharing this particular printer on the network, only users with a username and password can print to it. That's the way printer sharing is configured on this PC in the Network and Sharing Center. Note you can change the behavior configured on your PC by clicking Network And Sharing Center now or reconfiguring it later.

8. Click OK.

Figure 9-1 Share a printer on the Sharing tab.

SHARE A PRINTER WITH THE WINDOWS XP OPERATING SYSTEM

It may be inconvenient to move a printer from a Windows XP–based machine to a Windows Vista–based machine. The printer may be in an office or room that must have a printer in it, and you want the Windows Vista–based machine somewhere else. Whatever the case, if you need to share a printer connected to a Windows XP–based PC, follow these steps:

1. Click Start, Control Panel.

2. Click Printers And Faxes.

3. Right-click the printer to share, and click Sharing.

4. Select Share This Printer.

5. Type a name for the printer.

6. Click OK.

Add Drivers

With most printers, by default, drivers for x86-based PCs are installed when the printer is. However, not all PCs are x86-based; some are x64-based, and some are Itanium-based. You need to look at each computer on your network to see what type of processor it uses so you can install drivers if necessary.

UNDERSTAND TYPES OF PROCESSORS

The term *x86* is the name given to all the Intel microprocessor families, and it started with the 80286 computer processor in 1982. The x86 microprocessors include the 386, 486, 586, 686, and higher technologies, as well as the Pentium family of computer chips. Most computers on your network are most likely these technologies. x86 chips are used with 32-bit operating systems.

You'll find newer chip technologies in the x64 family. These 64-bit processors are from AMD and Intel and support the x64 extensions to the x86 architecture. You might have one of these types of processors if you recently purchased a high-end PC running Windows Vista Premium, Ultimate, or Business. x64 processors are compatible with 32-bit operating systems and hardware, but if a driver exists for x64, it should be installed.

Itanium is much different from x86 or x64 technology. Itanium is the brand name for 64-bit Intel microprocessors. Itanium's primary use is to support large applications that require more than 4 GB of memory. It is unlikely you have any Itanium-based computers at your home or small office.

FIND YOUR PROCESSOR TYPE

To find out what type of processor your computer uses, follow these steps:

1. Click Start, Computer, and select System Properties.

2. Under System, locate Processor.

3. In Figure 9-2, note that the processor is an Intel Core 2. Find out what your processor is here. Note that you can also see the manufacturer name, model, and Windows Experience rating, among other things.

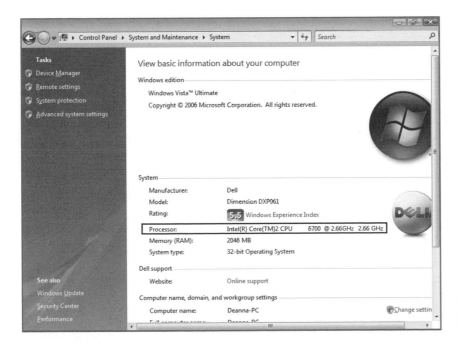

Figure 9-2
Find out what kind of processor your PC uses.

NOTE On Windows XP, click Start, right-click My Computer, and on the General tab, locate the processor type. If you don't see 64 anywhere, it's an x86 processor.

ADD A PRINTER DRIVER

To add a printer driver for any computer on your network, follow these steps:

1. Locate the printer in the Printers folder, and right-click the printer.

2. Select Run As Administrator, and select Sharing.

3. Click Continue.

4. If necessary, click Change Sharing Options.

5. Click Additional Drivers.

6. Select the driver to add, as shown in Figure 9-3.

7. Click OK.

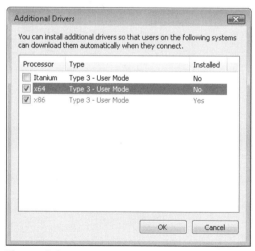

Figure 9-3 Select the drivers to add.

8. If prompted, insert the disk where the driver can be found, or click Browse to locate the driver. (If you don't have the driver available, click Cancel, visit the printer manufacturer's Web site, and then locate and download the driver you need. Return here, click Browse again, and locate the driver you downloaded to your PC.)

9. Work through the installation wizards if they appear.

10. Once installed, click Close.

Set Security Permissions

When you share a printer, default share setting are configured. The following permissions are created and configured automatically after you share a printer:

- Everyone who has access to the printer can print to it.
- Administrators can print, manage printers, and manage documents.
- The creator/owner can manage documents. The creator/owner is the person who installs the printer.

Understanding what these terms mean is important, and once you understand what printing, managing printers, and managing documents entail, you may want to give others on the network more or fewer permissions.

UNDERSTAND SHARE PERMISSIONS ON PRINTERS

Three Share permissions exist: Print, Manage Documents, and Manage Printers. There's also an option to apply Special Permissions, which I'll introduce only briefly:

Print By default, each user can print and then cancel, pause, or restart documents or files they send to the printer.

Manage Documents Users with this permission can manage print jobs in the print queue, including those created by other users on the network. This means users with this permission can cancel, pause, and resume other people's print jobs.

Manage Printers Users with this permission can rename, delete, share, and choose preferences for the printer. Users can set printer permissions for other users and manage all jobs in the print queue.

Special Permissions These permissions are generally reserved for system administrators and allow a user to change the printer owner. The Creator/Owner is the person who installed the printer.

> **CAUTION** Although you can set advanced NTFS permissions for printers, don't. Set advanced permissions only if the share permissions won't work for you. Mixing share and NTFS (advanced) permissions can result in problems with "effective" permissions later that will be difficult to diagnose.

CHANGE DEFAULT SHARE PERMISSIONS

If you want to change the default permissions for a printer, it's as simple as selecting Allow or Deny for the desired person or group on the Security tab in the printer's Properties dialog box. For instance, you might trust everyone on your network to use and manage the printer appropriately, and if those users need more access than the default Print permission, you can select other permissions as desired. You might also want to do this to avoid having to input administrator credentials to use the printer from another computer when logged on as a standard user.

To change the default share permissions, follow these steps:

1. Locate the printer in the Printers folder, right-click it, and select Run As Administrator.

2. Click Sharing.

3. Click Continue.

4. On the Security tab, under Group Or User Names, select Everyone.

5. In the Permissions For Everyone box, select Allow for Manage Printers and Manage Permissions. Do not select Special Permissions. See Figure 9-4.

6. Click OK.

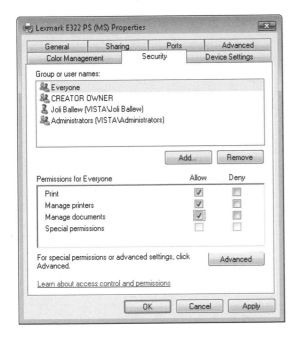

Figure 9-4 Allow permission for the Everyone group if desired.

REMOVE EVERYONE

If you don't want everyone who has access to the network to be able to print to your printer, you'll need to remove the Everyone group and configure users individually. This will require you to add each user separately who you want to give permission to print. This is a good way to go if you do not want your 6- and 12-year-old kids to print to the printer but you want your wife and grown son to be able to do so.

To remove the Everyone group, follow these steps:

1. Locate the printer in the Printers folder, right-click it, and select Run As Administrator.

2. Click Sharing.

3. Click Continue.

4. On the Security tab, under Group Or User Names, select Everyone.

5. Click Remove.

6. Click OK.

ADD USERS AND APPLY PERMISSIONS

To add users and apply permissions for each—for instance, you want to give limited permissions to your 15-year-old daughter with a new digital camera, and you want to give your wife full access—follow these steps:

1. Locate the printer in the Printers folder, right-click it, and select Run As Administrator.

2. Click Sharing.

3. Click Continue.

4. On the Security tab, under Group Or User Names, click Add.

5. Type the name of the user to add, and click Check Names. See Figure 9-5.

6. To add another user, type a semicolon, and repeat step 5.

7. Click OK.

8. On the Security tab, select the first user you added in step 5.

9. In Permissions, select the permission to apply.

10. Repeat steps 8 and 9 until all users have the required permissions.

11. Click OK.

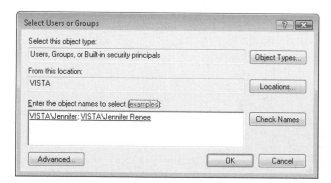

Figure 9-5 Add users separately to apply distinct permissions.

Configure Advanced Printer Settings

The printer settings you configure as an administrator are applied network-wide. This means if you configure your shared printer preferences to make the printer available only during specific times of the day, then users can access the printer only during those times (unless they have additional permissions or administrator credentials). Additionally, you can configure spool settings, keep all printed documents, turn on or off advanced printing features, and more.

What is available to configure depends somewhat on what your printer offers, though. For instance, you may be able to change how many copies to make for each print by default, the print quality, the scaling options, and Adobe PostScript options such as optimizing for speed or creating a negative output, as well as toner darkness, smoothing, and image quality. You'll need to browse through your printer options to find out exactly what's available.

CONFIGURE ADVANCED PRINTER SETTINGS

Advanced printer settings, those available on the Advanced tab in the printer's Properties dialog box, are the same no matter what printer is installed. See Figure 9-6. The printing defaults and additional printer settings for printers differ from manufacturer to manufacturer and from model to model.

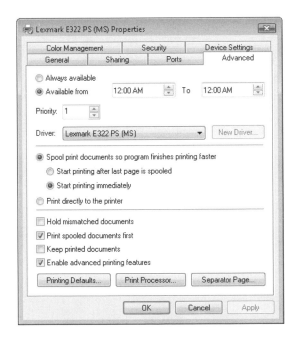

Figure 9-6 Advanced printer properties on the Advanced tab include the option to configure when the printer can be used and when it can't.

To make a change to any setting, simply apply the change by selecting or deselecting the appropriate radio button or option. You can also select Available From and configure when the printer can and cannot be used.

A few concepts you may not be familiar with include the following:

Spooling In print spooling, documents are loaded into a buffer (usually an area on a hard disk) and are held until the printer acquires the data and readies it for print. Spooling lets you send a number of print jobs to the queue instead of waiting for each one to finish before sending another.

Mismatched documents The printer holds the print jobs in the queue that don't match the setup for the printer, such as not having the right tray of paper attached to the printer.

Keep documents after they have printed The printer keeps documents that have printed in the queue in case you need to print them again.

Separator page The printer inserts a blank page at the beginning of each document to make it easier to find documents at the printer when multiple documents have printed.

For the most part, the default settings are the best, with the exception of limiting the times the printer can be used.

CONFIGURE PRINTING DEFAULTS

As noted, printing defaults differ from printer to printer. In Figure 9-6, shown in the previous section, note the Printing Defaults button. Click this button to access and change the shared printer's defaults. You'll likely be able to change the following:

- Orientation
- Page order
- Paper quality
- Paper source
- Paper size
- Print quality

More expensive printers have additional options. Browse the options available for your printer, and configure the settings as desired.

Access a Local Printer

Generally you'll print to a printer from an application such as a word processing, spreadsheet, database, or graphic imaging program. The option to print is frequently in the File menu, and often, an icon exists on a menu bar, a toolbar, or a separate pane in the interface. Figure 9-7 shows the Print option in Microsoft Office Word 2007.

Figure 9-7 In Office Word 2007, the Print options are located under the Microsoft Office Button in the toolbar.

Clicking Print almost always offers a Print dialog box (unless you perform a "quick" print), an example of which is shown in Figure 9-8. With administrator credentials, a user can change everything about the printer, including the printer properties and other options. Users with the ability to only print do not have these privileges, and administrator credentials are required to make changes.

It doesn't really matter what operating system you're using when accessing a printer; what matters is the ability to locate it. Shared printers will appear listed in the drop-down list and are easily accessible. Figure 9-9 shows an example. Here, Fax is selected.

You can also access shared printers that are connected to other PCs on the network by using the drop-down list shown in Figure 9-9, but you must manually add them first by using Control Panel. I detail how to do this next.

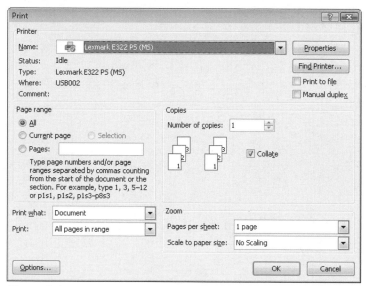

Figure 9-8 Print by using the Print dialog box.

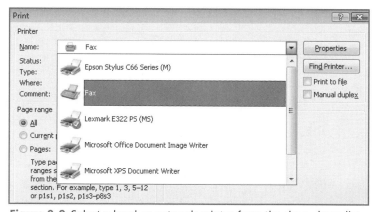

Figure 9-9 Select a local or network printer from the drop-down list.

TIP If you install Remote Desktop, detailed in Chapter 14, you'll be able to print to your network printer from anywhere, provided you have the proper configuration, credentials, and an Internet connection. For more information, refer to that chapter.

Add a Shared Printer Connected to Another PC

To access a printer connected to another PC on the network from your Windows Vista–based machine, you'll need to add it manually. You can achieve this through Control Panel, Hardware and Sound, and Printers.

To add a shared printer connected to another PC on your network, follow these steps:

1. On the PC running Windows Vista, click Start, click Control Panel, and under Hardware and Sound, click Printer.

2. In the toolbar, click Add Printer.

3. From the Add Printer dialog box, click Add A Network, Wireless Or Bluetooth printer. See Figure 9-10. Click Next.

4. Browse through the list to locate the printer to add. Figure 9-11 shows an example of a network with several computers and multiple printers. Select the printer, and click Next.

5. If prompted to install a driver, click Install Driver, and click Continue to proceed.

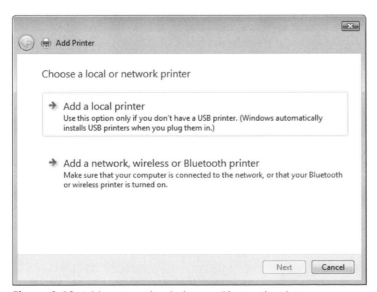

Figure 9-10 Add a network, wireless, or Bluetooth printer.

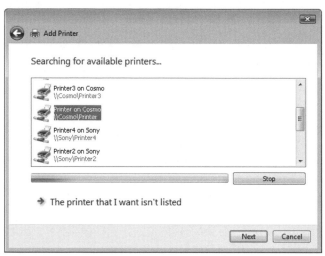

Figure 9-11 Select the printer to add.

6. Select or deselect Set As The Default Printer. (The default printer will always be selected by default, and all "quick" print jobs will automatically go to this printer.)

7. Click Next.

8. Click Finish.

The printer will now appear in all drop-down lists for printer options, and you'll access it in the same way you access local printers connected directly to your own PC.

> **TIP** To change which printer is the default, open the Printer folder, right-click the folder to configure as the default printer, and click Set As Default Printer.

Chapter Summary

In this chapter, you learned how to create, configure, manage, and access shared local and network printers. By networking printers, you can share the printer with other network users, reducing the need for multiple printers. You can also manage how and when others print documents and manage the printer from your own Windows Vista–based computer.

PART IV

Expanding the Network

CHAPTER 10

Create a Windows Home Server

- **Learn about Windows Home Server**
- **Understand system requirements**
- **Install and set up Windows Home Server software**
- **Configure settings for best performance**
- **Manage data**
- **Create and configure a backup strategy**

WINDOWS HOME SERVER is a hardware and software solution for storing, managing, and backing up the data on your home network. With Windows Home Server, you can recover from almost any disaster, even one that destroys all the data on every computer on your network! One of the best features of Windows Home Server, though, is that once it's set up, that's it. There's no need to keep a keyboard, mouse, or monitor connected to it, which makes it a great way to manage all the data without having to designate an entire desk or room to do it, and there's no need to interact with it to perform backups or other tasks after it has been configured. It's all done automatically.

With Windows Home Server, you can recover from almost any disaster, even one that destroys all the data on every computer on your network!

Understand What Windows Home Server Offers

Windows Home Server is an operating system much like Windows Vista. You can install programs and drivers on it, for instance, and even surf the Internet. You can use Microsoft Paint, get e-mail, and access and use items in the Accessories folder. Although Windows Home Server is an operating system and does offer many of the familiar applications you're used to seeing in operating systems, it wasn't created to be used as an ordinary PC. Windows Home Server, once set up, is designed to be used without a keyboard, mouse, or monitor and to act as a server for storing and managing your network data—and nothing else.

Windows Home Server will manage your network data for you. You can configure Windows Home Server to automatically back up data on every computer on your network and use it to securely access your files and folders. You can even add more hard drives to it if you need extra space. Of course, as easy as it is to back up data, it's equally simple to restore if a disaster strikes. And, you can restore entire computers or only a few lost files. Additionally, your home server comes preconfigured with shared folders for photos, music, videos, and the like, and you get to specify who can access what, just like you can on any PC equipped with the Windows Vista operating system.

Windows Home Server also monitors itself. It ensures backups are being performed regularly, keeps two copies of shared data if space allows for it, and collects security information from Windows Vista–based PCs on the network to centrally monitor the health of the PCs on the network. You can access the server remotely by using a Web browser on another computer, too. This lets you access shared folders, applications, printers, and more, from anywhere you can obtain access to the Internet.

Finally, you can stream media throughout your home by using the Windows Home Server Console. You can turn on media library sharing so that media can be accessed from an Xbox 360 or compatible digital media receiver attached to your home network.

Installation takes about an hour of your own time (the actual installation process could take several hours in total), but it's really straightforward. A wizard walks you through the installation process, and once installed, the Windows Home Server Console makes configuring the server a breeze. However, it's important you understand and meet the minimum requirements for the hardware and network, that you make the physical connection properly, and that you install the software with the options on each computer on your network.

Know the System Requirements

The hardware you choose for your home server must meet minimum system requirements. For the most part, the more you can improve on these minimum requirements, the better the performance. Since this is a long-term data management solution, try to meet the recommended requirements listed in the "Hardware Requirements" section; you'll be depending on this server for some time and want it to be as powerful and reliable as possible. Keep in mind that you'll need only a monitor, keyboard, and mouse during installation and setup, so there's no need to improve on those items. In addition to hardware requirements, the PC you select to act as the server must meet operating system version requirements too.

HARDWARE REQUIREMENTS

The PC you select to act as your Windows Home Server must meet minimum requirements. Minimum hardware requirements for installing Windows Home Server are as follows:

CPU 1GHz Pentium 3 or better

RAM 512 MB or more

Hard drive A 70-GB internal hard drive (IDE, ATA, SATA, or SCSI)

DVD A bootable DVD drive

Network interface card (NIC) 100-Mbps Ethernet

Motherboard ACPI-compliant and Windows Server 2003–compliant

You'll also need a monitor, standard (QWERTY) keyboard, and mouse or compatible pointing device.

If you want to improve performance, try to meet these recommended requirements:

CPU 2 GHz or better

RAM 1 GB or higher

Hard drive A 70-GB hard drive for Windows Home Server and two 70-GB drives (or larger) for storage

DVD A bootable DVD drive

Network interface card (NIC) 100-Mbps Ethernet

Motherboard ACPI-compliant and Windows Server 2003–compliant

You'll also need a monitor, QWERTY keyboard, and mouse or compatible pointing device.

> **NOTE** Laptops are not supported for Windows Home Server.

NETWORK REQUIREMENTS

Your network must also meet the following network requirements:

- The server must connect to the network by using a 100-Mbps (or faster) wired connection.

- The connection to the Internet must be through broadband.

- There must be an external broadband router/firewall device with a 100-Mbps (or faster) wired Ethernet connection.

- PCs on the network obtain their IP addresses from the router/firewall device on the network.

NOTE You must use an Ethernet cable to connect your server to your broad-band router. Wirelessly connecting your server to your broadband router or switch is not supported.

OPERATING SYSTEM REQUIREMENTS

The computer you select to run Windows Home Server must be running one of the following operating systems:

- Windows Vista Home Basic
- Windows Vista Home Premium
- Windows Vista Business
- Windows Vista Enterprise
- Windows Vista Ultimate
- Windows XP Home with Service Pack 2 (SP2)
- Windows XP Professional with SP2
- Windows XP Media Center Edition 2005 with SP2 and rollup 2
- Windows XP Media Center Edition 2005 with SP2
- Windows XP Media Center Edition 2004 with SP2
- Windows XP Tablet Edition with SP2
- Windows Home Server Connector Software CD

NOTE While installing Windows Home Server, your hard drive will be formatted, meaning all data on the drive will be lost. Make sure you back up any data you want to keep prior to installation.

Run Windows Home Server Setup

Once you've met the minimum requirements, all you have to do to get started is make the Ethernet connection to the existing network, power on, and run the Windows Home Server setup. Make sure you use a wired Ethernet connection to your network. Disconnect any external USB or Apple FireWire drives too; you can reconnect those drives after setup is complete.

When you're ready to start installation, insert the Windows Home Server DVD into the drive, restart the computer, and boot to the DVD. When you see the Welcome screen, you're ready to begin.

To install Windows Home Server, follow these steps:

1. Insert the Windows Home Server DVD, reboot, and press the appropriate key on the keyboard to boot to the DVD. Wait while the files load.

2. At the Welcome screen, click Next to begin.

3. On the Load Additional Storage Drivers page, verify all your hard drives appear on this page. If they do not, click Load Drivers to load additional drivers and add the missing drives. Click Next.

> **TIP** If a message appears that no hard drive is found that is capable of hosting Windows Home Server, you'll need to browse to the location of the hard disk driver. If you aren't sure where that driver is stored, use Device Manager to obtain the properties for the drive and the location of the drivers.

4. On the Select An Installation Type page, select New Installation, and click Next. Note that all data on the drive will be erased. If you have not backed up all the data you want to keep, click Cancel to end the installation.

5. On the Select Your Regional And Keyboard Settings page, select the format of your time and currency, and select the language of your keyboard or input method. Then click Next.

6. On the End-User License Agreement page, review the end-user license agreement. To continue, click I Accept This Agreement, and then click Next.

7. On the Enter Your Windows Home Server Product Key page, type your Windows Home Server product key, and then click Next.

8. On the Name Your Home Server page, type a name for your home server, and then click Next.

9. If prompted to disconnect external drives, do so.

10. Review the Formatting Hard Drives page. To continue, click I Acknowledge That All Data On These Drives Will Be Lost, and then click Next. To confirm that you want to continue, click Yes.

11. On the Ready To Install Windows Home Server page, click Start. The Windows Home Server documentation states that this step may take several hours to complete. Your home server will reboot multiple times during setup. No additional input is required from you during this time.

TIP During each reboot, you'll see the option to boot to CD or DVD. Don't do this, or the setup will start over!

12. When Windows Home Server boots for the first time, click Welcome.

13. Type a password, confirm the password, and type a password hint. Make sure you read and understand the requirements for creating a strong password. It needs to be at least seven characters and include uppercase and lowercase letters, as well as numbers and/or symbols. Click the right arrow to continue.

14. On the Help Protect Windows Home Server Automatically page, click On or Off next. The recommended setting is On to keep Windows Home Server up-to-date. Click the right arrow to continue.

15. On the Customer Experience Improvement Program page, determine whether you want to participate in this program, and click Yes or No. Click the right arrow to continue.

16. On the Windows Error Reporting page, decide whether you want to automatically send error reports to Microsoft, and click Yes or No. Click the right arrow to continue.

17. If setup did not automatically install a driver for your network card, the fol-
    lowing message appears:

    Make sure your home server is connected to the network and that you have
    the appropriate drivers for your network card. To install the correct driver,
    follow the instructions in "Adding Drivers for Your Network Card" in Trouble-
    shooting Setup before you shut down your home server.

18. Click Continue.

19. Click Start, and select Log off.

20. Restart the computer, and log on. Later, you'll log off and disconnect the
    monitor, mouse, and keyboard.

Verify you can connect to the Internet from the new Windows Home Server. If you
cannot, refer to the "Troubleshoot" section next.

Troubleshoot

You must be able to connect to your network and the Internet before continuing. You
can perform several tasks if you are having trouble accessing your network or the
Internet, including verifying your workgroup name, creating a new connection, and
using Device Manager to update an Ethernet adapter, controller, or similar device.

VERIFY WORKGROUP NAME

Your new Windows Home Server will need to have a unique computer name on your
existing network and be able to connect to it. Before continuing, verify that the
computer name and workgroup name are correct. If they are not correct, make
changes as noted here.

To verify the computer and workgroup name are configured correctly, follow
these steps:

1. Log on to Windows Home Server.

2. Click Start, and right-click My Computer.

3. Select Properties.

4. On the Computer Name tab, note the computer name. No other computer on the network should have that name. Also, note the workgroup name. This computer needs to be configured with the same workgroup name as your existing network. If either of these needs to be changed, click Change.

5. In the Computer Name Changes dialog box, type the desired computer name and workgroup name. Click OK.

6. Click OK, OK, and OK again.

7. Click Yes to restart the PC.

NOTE You have 30 days to activate Windows Home Server after installation is complete. If you do not activate within 30 days, you cannot continue to use Windows Home Server. You can activate Windows Home Server from the Resources page on Windows Home Server Settings or via the pop-up that appears in the taskbar.

Before continuing, verify you can access the Internet from the Windows Home Server PC. If you cannot, work through the next section.

RUN THE NEW CONNECTION WIZARD

If you can't connect to the Internet, you might need to run the New Connection Wizard. To create a new connection by using this wizard, follow these steps:

1. From the Windows Home Server PC, click Start, Control Panel, Network Connections, and New Connection Wizard.

2. On the Welcome To The New Connection Wizard page, click Next.

3. Click Connect to the Internet. Click Next.

4. Select Connect Using A Broadband Connection That Is Always On. Click Next.

5. Click Finish.

UPDATE AN ETHERNET DRIVER IN DEVICE MANAGER

You will not be able to connect to your network or the Internet if your Ethernet adapter isn't working properly. To see whether your Ethernet adapter or controller is causing a problem, open Device Manager:

1. From the Windows Home Server PC, Click Start, right-click My Computer, and click Properties.

2. From the Hardware tab, click Device Manager.

3. Look for any red *X*s or yellow question marks in the list. Figure 10-1 shows a problematic Ethernet controller.

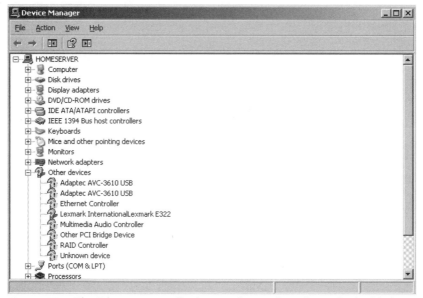

Figure 10-1 The Ethernet controller has a yellow exclamation point beside it. The driver for this controller needs to be installed.

4. Double-click the device that is not working, and from the Properties dialog box, select Driver.

5. Click Update Driver.

6. Select Install The Software Automatically (Recommended), and click Next.

7. If a driver is found, click Next to install it. If a driver is not found, you'll need to obtain the driver some other way. This may include browsing to a driver disk that came with your PC, downloading a compatible driver from the Internet, or waiting for Windows Update to offer a driver to you at a future date.

Configure Windows Home Server Settings

After installing Windows Home Server, you need to install the Windows Home Server Connector software. The Windows Home Server Connector software does the following:

- It regularly looks at the health of your home computer.
- It connects your networked computers to Windows Home Server.
- It backs up your home computers daily.
- It lets you to remotely administer Windows Home Server.

To install the Windows Home Server software, follow these steps:

1. Insert the Windows Home Server Connector CD into a computer that is connected to your home network. The Windows Home Server Connector Wizard will start. Click Next to continue. See Figure 10-2.

Figure 10-2 Install the Windows Home Server Connector software.

2. On the End-User License Agreement page, review the end-user license agreement. To continue, click I Accept This Agreement, and then click Next.

3. Wait while the software locates your new Windows Home Server PC.

4. Enter the password for the Windows Home Server. Click Next.

5. After installation and configuration is complete, click Next to continue.

If you see a pop-up message in the Notification area saying that Windows Home Server does not recognize the account on the computer you just installed the connector software on, you'll need to create an account for the user on the Windows Home Server PC. You also need to run the Windows Home Server Connector Wizard on all your other home computers to connect them to Windows Home Server. Make sure to run the wizard on only one computer at a time.

> **NOTE** If you do not have your Connector CD, you can install the Connector software from the Software shared folder on Windows Home Server.

Manage Windows Home Server

With everything installed, you can now start personalizing Windows Home Server. You'll need to create user accounts for everyone on your network and familiarize yourself with the shared folders on the new server. You'll also want to browse the options in the Windows Home Server Console, where you can view computers and backups, server storage, the health of the network, and more.

USER ACCOUNTS

User accounts let Windows Home Server know that it's all right for the people on your network to access the shared folders on the new server. Without a user account configured on the server itself, users won't be able to access the shared data on it.

To add a user account, follow these steps:

1. From any networked computer with Windows Home Server Connector software installed, right-click the Windows Home Server icon in the Notification area of the taskbar.

2. Click Windows Home Server Console. See Figure 10-3.

3. Type the password, and click the right arrow to proceed. The Window Home Console opens, and you have access to the Windows Home Console on the server. What you see here is exactly what you'd see if you logged on to the server itself and opened the console from the Windows Home Server PC.

4. Click the User Accounts tab. See Figure 10-4.

Figure 10-3 The Windows Home Server Console option is available in the Notification area of any PC with the Windows Home Server Connector software installed.

Figure 10-4
The User Accounts tab.

5. Click Add, and work through the User Account Wizard. You'll need to type the following:

   - First name and optionally a last name.

   - Logon name. (Use the same logon name used on other computers; it's best if they match. If they don't, users will be prompted each time they log on.)

   - If you want the user to have remote access to the server. Remote access lets you use a Web browser to access your Windows Home Server files when you are away from home.

   - Password. (Use the same password associated with the logon name used on other computers; it's best if they match. If they don't, users will be prompted each time they log on.)

   - Access to shared folders (Full, Read, or None).

6. Click Done.

7. Repeat for the other users on your network computers.

SHARED FOLDERS

Shared folders let you store data on your new server so that others on the network can access them easily. Several shared folders are already created for you:

- Photos

- Music

- Videos

- Software

- Public

- A personal shared folder for each user account

You can also add your own folders to share and thus further personalize Windows Home Server. To add your own shared folder and view shared folders already created, follow these steps:

1. From any networked computer with Windows Home Server Connector software installed, right-click the Windows Home Server icon in the Notification area of taskbar.

2. Click Windows Home Server Console.

3. Type the password, and click the right arrow to proceed. The Windows Home Console opens, and you have access to the Windows Home Console on the server. What you see here is exactly what you'd see if you logged on to the server itself and opened the console from the Windows Home Server PC.

4. Click the Shared Folders tab. See Figure 10-5.

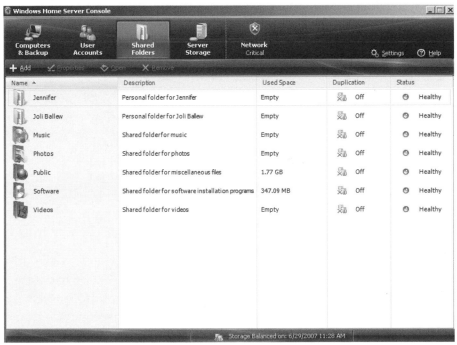

Figure 10-5 Add a shared folder from the Shared Folders tab in the Windows Home Server Console.

5. Click Add.

6. Type a name for the server and, optionally, a description. Click Enable Folder Duplication if you have multiple hard drives. (Folder Duplication folders are duplicated across multiple drives, and if one drive fails, you have a secondary backup.) Click Next.

7. Choose the level of access for each user. You can choose from Full, Read, or None. See Figure 10-6.

8. Click Finish. Click Done.

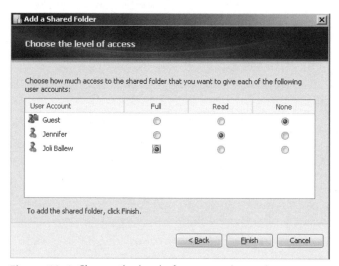

Figure 10-6 Choose the level of access each user has to your new shared folder.

Configure the Backup Settings

By default, all the hard drives on all your home computers will be backed up every night between midnight and 6 a.m. You might just want to leave that setting the way it is. You can customize these settings in the Windows Home Server Console by using the Settings option if you want, though. Additionally, the Windows Home Server Console offers an easy way to view the backups that have taken place, to back up any computer right now, and to configure what a backup should contain.

To view backup options, follow these steps:

1. From any networked computer with Windows Home Server Connector software installed, right-click the Windows Home Server icon in the Notification area of the taskbar.

2. Click Windows Home Server Console.

3. Type the password, and click the right arrow to proceed.

4. Click the Computers & Backup tab.

5. Click View Backups. From here you can do the following:

    a. View the backups that have taken place.

    b. Keep or delete a backup.

    c. Learn how to restore files from backup.

    d. Learn more about backup management and backup cleanup.

6. Click Backup Now. From here you can do the following:

    a. Enter a name for the manual backup.

    b. Perform a manual backup.

7. Select a computer from the list of computers available on the Computers & Backups tab. Click Configure Backup. From here you can do the following:

    a. Add files and folders to back up that are not configured automatically, such as Documents, Pictures, Music, and the like.

    b. Select the volumes to back up if more than one exists.

8. Click Settings, and click the Backup tab in the Windows Home Server Settings dialog box, as shown in Figure 10-7.

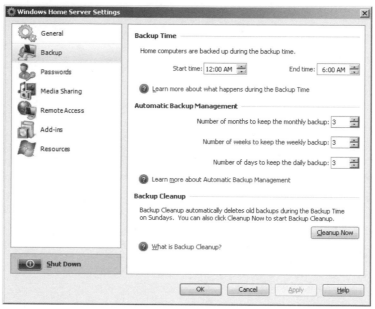

Figure 10-7 Backup settings.

9. On the Backup tab in the Windows Home Server Settings dialog box, you can do the following:

a. Change the start and end time the backup occurs.

b. Change the amount of time to keep the backups.

c. Perform a backup cleanup (which deletes old backups that aren't needed).

Configure the Windows Home Server Settings

As shown in Figure 10-7, the Settings dialog box offers lots of tabs for configuring how Windows Home Server should perform. There are several categories, each of them listed here with their options defined:

- General
  - Configure the date and time.
  - Configure the regional settings.

- Configure Windows Update.

- Configure Customer Experience Improvement Program.

- Configure Windows error reporting.

- Passwords

  - Change the Windows Home Server password.

  - Configure the User Accounts Password Policy.

- Media Sharing

  - Enable streaming of Music, Photos, and Videos shared folders so that you can stream digital media from Windows Home Server to a device that supports Windows Media Connect.

- Remote Access

  - Configure Web site connectivity.

  - Configure your broadband router.

  - Configure your domain name.

  - Configure the settings for your Windows Home Server Web site.

- Add-ins

  - Install and uninstall Windows Home Server add-ins.

  - View available add-ins.

- Resources

  - Activate Windows Home Server.

  - View hardware information about your home server.

  - View Windows Home Server version information.

  - Learn more about Windows Home Server.

  - Connect to the Windows Home Server community.

  - Contact product support.

Finally, you can shut down Windows Home Server from the Settings dialog box by clicking Shut Down. For more information about Windows Home Server Settings, click Help in the Windows Home Server Console.

View the Home Network Health

There's one last item to review before moving on, and that's the Network icon in the Windows Home Server Console. This icon offers a visual reference about how healthy your network is. Figure 10-8 shows that the network health is critical. Clicking the Network Critical icon opens the screen shown in Figure 10-9, which notes here that one of the computers on the network does not have antivirus software installed. Anytime you see a critical icon, review the information, and see whether the problem can be resolved. If it cannot or if you want to ignore it, select Ignore This Issue.

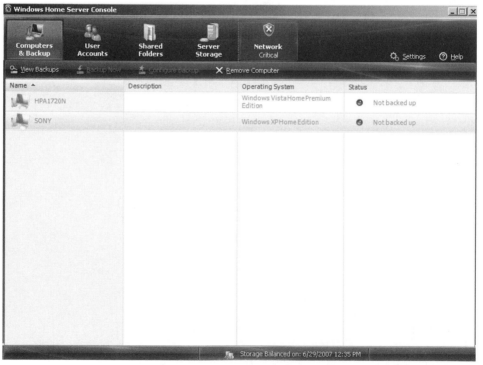

Figure 10-8 Network Critical means something needs your attention right away.

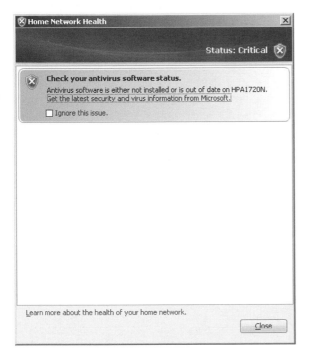

Figure 10-9 Network notifications like these let you know exactly what's wrong.

Explore Additional Features

Windows Home Server comes with additional features you might want to explore by clicking Start, All Programs; these include Administrative Tools, Remote Assistance, and Remote Access. With these tools you can further personalize your Windows Home Server PC, access the PC from anywhere you can gain Internet access through a Web browser, and perform such tasks as setting local security policies, looking at performance logs, and viewing items collected in Event Viewer.

Chapter Summary

In this chapter, you learned how to install and configure a Windows Home Server PC and how to connect your home network's PCs to it. Once installed and configured, you learned how to back up data automatically, use the Windows Home Server Console, and configure server settings.

CHAPTER 11

Work with Offline Files

- **Understand offline files**
- **Enable offline files**
- **Configure Sync Center**
- **Manage sync conflicts**
- **Create sync partnerships**

MOST PEOPLE who use a laptop in an office setting store their critical data on a company server or network share. The reason is because a network share makes it easy to store data and back it up regularly, and it makes the data available from anywhere you can obtain access to the network (such as through the company's intranet or the World Wide Web).

If you use a laptop at work (or work from several different offices toting a laptop to and from each), you'll appreciate the offline files feature in the Windows Vista operating system. With offline files, you can take data that's stored on a network drive with you, modify it, and then sync it back to the server on reconnection. Offline files also work

You can't always be connected to the network share, for instance, when you're on an airplane or simply away from a broadband or wireless Internet connection.

for home users. You can sync your mobile phone or pocket PC with your desktop PC in the same manner. Because all this happens automatically and behind the scenes, you hardly ever have to think about it once it's set up.

Understand Offline Files

Offline files let you access data stored on a shared network folder even when the network share is not available. You can't always be connected to the network share, for instance, when you're on an airplane or simply away from a broadband or wireless Internet connection.

When you enable offline files, you choose the folders to make available when you're not connected to the network. You select specific folders (and their subfolders), and a copy of the data is saved automatically to your mobile computer. You can then work on the files even if you aren't connected to the network. When you reconnect, the files are synced so that what's on the network share matches what is on your local hard disk. Additionally, syncing files automatically redirects any open files to the online copy of them.

> **TIP** Offline files also let you continue working if your network becomes disabled or your connection to it fails. Just continue to work as usual, and when you can connect again, your files will automatically be synced.

Turn On the Offline Files Feature

To use offline files, you must turn on the feature and select the folders to copy and sync. You must also decide what to do when sync conflicts occur and create sync partnerships between computers. Let's start by turning on the offline files feature.

To locate offline files settings and turn the feature on, follow these steps:

1. Click Start, and in the Start Search box, type **Offline Files**.

2. In the Start menu results, under Programs, select Offline Files.

3. On the General tab, shown in Figure 11-1, click Enable Offline Files.

4. Click Continue.

5. Click OK.

6. Click Yes to restart your computer.

Figure 11-1 Click Enable Offline Files to get started.

Select Offline Files

To be able to work with a file offline, you must make that file available by copying it to your own hard drive. To select files and folders for offline use, follow these steps:

1. Click Start, Network.

2. Select the network computer that stores the shared file or folder you want to make available offline. The computer you choose does not need to be running Windows Vista.

3. Right-click the file or folder, and click Always Available Offline. See Figure 11-2.

4. Wait while the files are prepared, shown in Figure 11-3. When the process finishes, click Close.

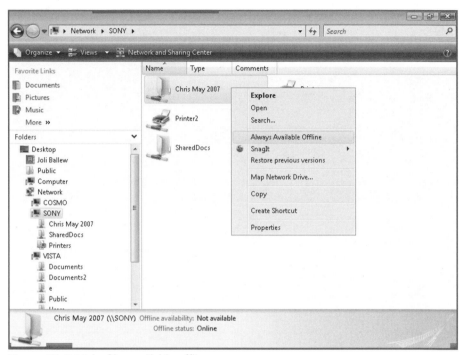

Figure 11-2 Make files available offline.

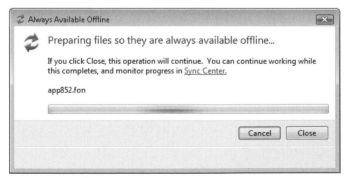

Figure 11-3 Wait while the files are prepared.

To verify the files have been prepared correctly, right-click the file or folder again, and make sure there's a check mark beside Always Available Offline. You'll also see an icon like the one shown in Figure 11-4 beside the folder you enabled.

Figure 11-4 This icon indicates a shared offline folder.

Work Offline

If you need to work offline because you are away from the network, because the network is down, because the network is slow, or because of any other reason, you'll need to specify you indeed want to work offline.

To work offline by manually selecting the option, follow these steps:

1. Click Start, Network.

2. Locate the folder containing the files you previously made available offline, and select it.

3. From the toolbar, click Work Offline. See Figure 11-5.

4. When finished working offline, click Work Online on the toolbar.

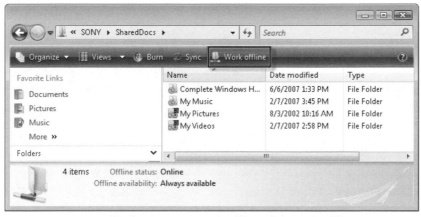

Figure 11-5 To specifically choose to work offline, click Work Offline.

If you aren't sure whether you're working offline or online, open the network folder you are working on, and look at the details pane at the bottom of the window. If it says Online, you're working online; if it says Offline, you're working offline.

> **TIP** To see all the available offline files, click Start, and in the Start Search box type **Offline Files**. Click Offline Files, click the General tab, and click View Your Offline Files.

Learn About Sync Center and Synchronization

You use Sync Center to keep your offline data in sync with your online data. You can sync data between your computer and portable music players, portable video players, personal digital assistants (PDAs), mobile phones, and Windows Mobile devices. You can also sync between your computer and network folders and compatible programs.

With Sync Center, you can be certain you are always using the most up-to-date files available. This means you're using the most recent version with the most recent changes. And it doesn't matter on what type of device you made the changes as long as you use Sync Center to keep it all synced up!

UNDERSTAND TYPES OF SYNCHRONIZATIONS

Syncing can be a one-way street or a two-way street. In a one-way sync, every time you modify a file in one location, the same information is synced with the data in the other. No changes are ever made to the first location, because the sync "boss" is, well, the boss of all changes!

In two-way sync, files are copied to and from both locations. Any modifications made on either device, the PC or the mobile device, are synced with the other. This is the most common sync setup.

You can open Sync Center by clicking Start, All Programs, Accessories, Sync Center.

UNDERSTAND HOW SYNC WORKS

When files are synchronized, Sync Center compares the files in both locations to see what has changed. If Sync Center finds that files differ, it syncs them. Although you don't have to understand all the particulars of what happens during the sync process, you need to understand the basics so you can make an informed decision regarding setting up sync partnerships and resolving sync conflicts.

Keep the following in mind when working with offline files and syncing data:

- If two files are compared and neither has been modified, no sync occurs for those files.

- If you add a file to one location, it will be added to the other.

- If you delete a file from one location, it will be deleted to the other.

- If one file has changes and one does not, the most recently changed version is selected and synced to the other location.

- If both files have been changed, a sync conflict occurs. You must manually select the version to keep.

NOTE Music can be synced by using Sync Center, but more often, Windows Media Player 11 is used instead. Windows Media Player was created with music in mind, specifically for music management; thus, it is programmed to be the default music sync application.

Use Sync Center and Offline Files

After turning on, selecting, and working with offline files, open Sync Center to see what's going on in there. You'll see an icon for offline files, which you can manually sync, view results for, view conflicts for, and resolve reported errors. Figure 11-6 shows Sync Center and the Offline Files icon.

Figure 11-6 After turning on and using offline files, you'll see the Offline Files icon in Sync Center.

CAUTION You cannot sync with network folders with Windows Vista Starter, Windows Vista Home Basic, or Windows Vista Home Premium. However, with these editions, you can sync with devices as previously mentioned.

MANUALLY SYNC OFFLINE FILES

Although you can let the sync process happen automatically (each time you access the network or share), you can also sync manually. You should sync manually any-time you are connected and want to verify a sync has taken place or want to view conflicts and errors.

To manually sync offline files, follow these steps:

1. Click Start, and in the Start Search box, type **Sync Center**.

2. Press Enter.

3. Click Sync.

If all goes well, the sync process will start and end without incident. However, you may get errors, warnings, and conflicts that will need to be handled. To see whether the sync process worked as desired, click View Sync Results in the Tasks pane. Figure 11-7 shows Sync Center with View Sync Results selected. There are several problems shown.

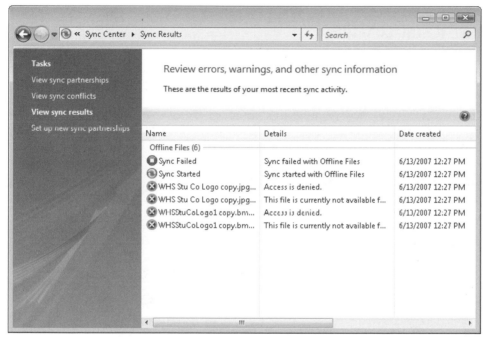

Figure 11-7 You may see problems when viewing sync results.

DEAL WITH SYNC ERRORS

Errors occur when a problem prevents a sync process from taking place. This occurs when the mobile device is not connected, not plugged in, or not turned on when you try to sync to it. An error also occurs when the computer you want to sync to is unavailable. Errors usually prevent a sync process from occurring.

DEAL WITH SYNC WARNINGS

Warnings are similar to errors but far less severe. A sync will continue to run through warnings; however, warnings can be the cause of a future error if not corrected. This can range from low laptop power to a phone that needs to be recharged.

DEAL WITH SYNC CONFLICTS

Sync conflicts occur when Sync Center can't decide what it should do regarding what file to keep. When two copies of a file exist and changes are made to both, Sync Center asks you to decide which file to keep. To resolve a conflict, click View Sync Conflicts in Sync Center, and click Resolve. You can also choose to ignore, or skip, the conflicted file. You can also choose to keep both files by renaming one of them.

CREATE A SCHEDULE TO SYNC OFFLINE FILES

To create a schedule to sync files and folders, open Sync Center, and select Offline Files. Click Schedule, as shown in Figure 11-8, and work through the wizard to create the sync schedule.

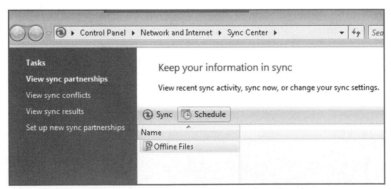

Figure 11-8 Click Schedule, and work through the wizard to create a sync schedule.

Create a Sync Partnership

With Sync Center you can create sync partnerships between your PC and your mobile devices. Creating a sync partnership lets you sync your data with different types of mobile devices that you connect via USB cable.

The first time you plug a Windows Mobile device into a computer that is connected to the Internet and running Windows Vista, Windows Mobile Device Center will automatically download and install. After you set up your device to sync in Windows Mobile Device Center, the sync results will appear in Sync Center. Setting up Windows Mobile Device Center takes only a few minutes and is a one-time process. If for some reason you are not prompted to install and run Windows Mobile Device Center, continue with the steps detailed next. If you cannot locate your device in Sync Center, you'll need to download and install Windows Mobile Device Center manually.

To see your mobile device in Sync Center and set it up if necessary, follow these steps:

1. Connect your mobile device to the PC, and turn it on. If prompted to install Windows Mobile Device Center, follow the directions to do so.

2. Open Sync Center.

3. In the Tasks pane, select View Sync Partnerships. If your mobile device is there, you're finished. If not, continue with step 4 through 7 here.

4. Click Set Up New Sync Partnerships.

5. Click the device in the list of available partnerships. (If you do not see the device, it may not be compatible, or you may not have installed Windows Mobile Device Center. Visit the manufacturer's Web site for updated drivers, download and install Windows Mobile Device Center, configure it, and then restart your computer. Start again at step 1.)

6. In the toolbar, click Set Up.

7. Select the settings and schedule to state how and when to sync the device.

Figure 11-9 shows a connected PDA. Note that choices for the PDA are Sync and Browse. Once synced, click View Sync Results to see the outcome. Figure 11-10 shows this.

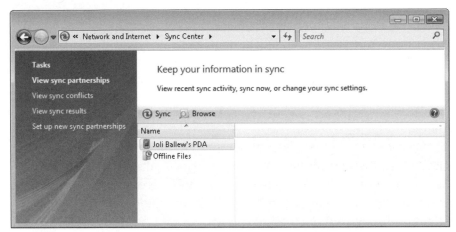

Figure 11-9 A successful installation of a PDA is shown in View Sync Partnerships.

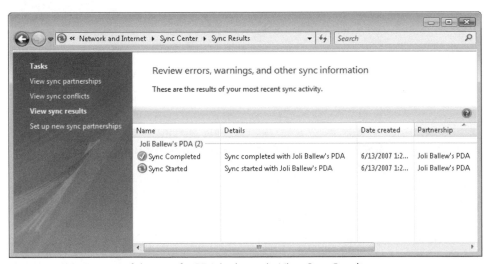

Figure 11-10 A successful sync of a PDA is shown in View Sync Results.

Chapter Summary

In this chapter, you learned all you need to know to get started with offline files. With only a basic understanding of the technology, you can work on network data even when away from the network. Upon reconnection, data will be automatically synced. You can also store and edit data by using pocket PCs, cell phones, and other mobile devices.

CHAPTER 12

Add an Xbox 360

- **Understand what a media extender offers**
- **Meet or exceed minimum and network requirements**
- **Make the physical connection**
- **Configure the extender**
- **Stream media to the extender**

A MEDIA EXTENDER is a device that streams media across your network. With a media extender such as an Xbox 360 and a PC with the Windows Vista operating system, you can watch media stored on your PC anywhere in your home by incorporating your wired or wireless network connection. Media can include videos, music, and pictures, among other things. All it takes is the proper hardware, a solid network, and a bit of configuration.

With a media extender such as an Xbox 360 and a PC with the Windows Vista operating system, you can watch media stored on your PC anywhere in your home by incorporating your wired or wireless network connection.

Opt for the Xbox

Although several types of media extenders exist, the Xbox 360 and its successors are my favorite. Of course, you can use the Xbox 360 to play games, but it's also capable of displaying media on high-end home-theater equipment, big-screen HDTVs, and similar home-theater hardware. Because you can use the Xbox 360 to access media stored on your Windows Vista–based PC, the media you access will look and feel just the way it does when you're sitting in front of your PC. There's nothing new to learn and no new skills to acquire. Just connect it, and enjoy!

NOTE To use the Xbox 360 as a media extender, you'll need to connect the console to a PC powered by Windows Media Center. Windows Media Center comes installed only on Windows Vista Home Premium and Windows Vista Ultimate.

Meet Network Requirements

A fast—100 megabits per second (Mbps) or faster—wired network is the best kind of network to use when connecting an Xbox to use as a media extender. A high-speed wired network provides only slight interference, provides maximum speed, and is often more reliable than a wireless network.

If you can't or don't want to run a wired connection to your Xbox 360, wireless is your second option. The problem with wireless networks and the Xbox 360 is that cordless phones and microwave ovens can interfere with the wireless signals needed by your network and may cause connections to fail or become sluggish. If you must use wireless, though, and can choose from the wireless standards, 802.11a is recommended not only because it is faster than 802.11b but also because it operates on a separate frequency from cell phones and the like.

Connect the Xbox 360 to the Network

You must connect your Xbox 360 to your network. If you have a wired network, just about all you have to do to connect it is to plug in the Ethernet cable that connects the Xbox 360 to your home network and plug the Xbox 360's power cord into a wall outlet. To be thorough, though, it's best to follow the step-by-step instructions included with the Xbox 360 if you aren't sure.

If you are connecting to a wireless network, you may need to configure wireless security and other settings on the Xbox 360 first. You'll be prompted regarding what you need to input, which may include Wired Equivalent Privacy (WEP) keys and Wi-Fi Protected Access (WPA) passphrases. A red light indicates it's ready to connect. Once you have the green light, the adapter is on and is connected to a wireless access point. If you need help, refer to the documentation included with your Xbox or go to *www.xbox.com*.

Configure the Xbox 360

After you have connected the Xbox 360 to the home network, turn it on. Then, work from the Media tab in the menu that's offered:

1. On the Media tab, select Media Center.

2. When prompted to connect the Xbox 360 to a PC with Media Center on your network, select A to continue. Note that if the Xbox 360 is connected to an 802.11b or 802.11g wireless network, you may be warned that poor performance can result. You should switch to a higher-performance wireless network (such as 802.11a) if your wireless router supports it. Be careful, though, because other devices on your network may not support 802.11a. Select Continue, and press A (Select) to continue.

3. Once connected, write down the Media Center setup key displayed on the screen. This code ensures that the Xbox 360 connects only with your Windows Vista–based PC, not any other on the network.

4. Press A to continue.

Configure the Windows Vista–Based PC

With the Xbox 360 connected to the network and with a Media Center setup key in hand, return to your Windows Vista–based PC. Click Start, and click Media Center. If you're prompted that the Xbox has been found on the network, click Yes, and skip to step 3.

To add an extender by using Windows Media Center, follow these steps:

1. Click Start, All Programs, Media Center.

2. Scroll down to Tasks, and then scroll right to Add Extender. Click Next to continue.

3. Type the eight-digit setup key displayed by the Xbox 360.

4. Click Next to continue.

5. Click Yes to see the media folders on your extender. Click Next.

6. Wait while the setup completes.

7. If prompted, click Yes (Recommended) to run the network performance tuner. Click Next. (If you aren't prompted or do not want to tune the network now and you want to return to the option later from Media Center, click Tasks, click Settings, click Extender, select the extender, and click Tune Network.)

8. Select Bar View or Graph View. Click Next.

9. Make adjustments to create the best signal possible. If you cannot get a good wireless signal, connect with Ethernet.

10. Click Finish.

Media sharing must be turned on under Network and Sharing, and the network must be private for media sharing to work. When media sharing is on, people and devices on the network can access shared music, pictures, and video on the computer, and the computer can also find and access these types of media on the network. The network must also be private to protect your personal data from being shared with others who you do not want to have access. If you're unsure about any of this, click Start, click Network, and open the Network and Sharing Center. Verify that the Media Sharing option is set to On and that the network is set to Private, as shown in Figure 12-1.

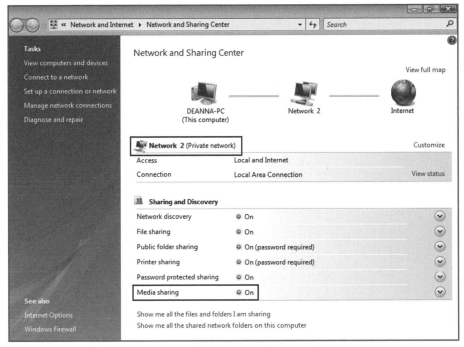

Figure 12-1 Make sure your network is private and media sharing is on.

TURN ON MEDIA SHARING IN WINDOWS MEDIA PLAYER 11

You can turn on media sharing in Media Player 11. To configure media sharing in this manner on the Windows Vista–based PC, follow these steps:

1. Click Start, All Programs, Windows Media Player.

2. Click the arrow under the Library button, and then click Media Sharing. Windows Media Player 11 lists all devices that have been allowed or denied access to your media library.

3. To access your media library from the Xbox 360, click it, and then click Allow. A green check mark appears after you allow the device to access your media library. See Figure 12-2.

Figure 12-2 If you see this exclamation point in the yellow triangle, click the icon, and select Allow.

Understand What Media Can Be Shared

You can share just about any media you have stored on your PC with others on your network and the media extender. These include but are not limited to the following:

- Protected Windows Media files downloaded from online stores.

- Music files, such as Windows Media Audio, MP3, and WAV files. You cannot share audio CDs inserted into the PC.

- Video files, such as Windows Media Video, AVI, MPEG-1, and MPEG-2. You cannot share DVD-Video discs inserted into the PC.

- Picture files, including JPEG and PNG.

- Playlists, such as Windows Media playlists and MP3 playlists.

Chapter Summary

In this chapter, you learned how and why you'd want to connect a media extender such as an Xbox 360 to your wired or wireless network. Having an extender lets you watch media stored on a Windows Vista–based PC anywhere in the house where you can connect the Xbox to a TV and the network. Installing an extender can help you "grow" your network and is a nice accessory.

CHAPTER 13

Access a Network Remotely

- **Understand remote access**
- **Meet system and network requirements**
- **Set up the host computer**
- **Select who can connect to the host PC**
- **Set up the guest computer**
- **Make the connection**
- **Configure advanced remote desktop settings**

YOU CAN ACCESS a PC at your home, and thus your network, even when you're away from home. Although you have several options for doing so, including a handful of them from third-party manufacturers, one of the best ways to access your computer remotely is by using the Remote Desktop feature of the Windows Vista operating system.

Remote Desktop not only lets you access a home-based PC and your home network, but it also brings the home computer's screen to yours. You may be in a hotel room, but once connected to your home PC by using Remote Desktop, your laptop's screen looks just like the computer

You may be in a hotel room, but once connected to your home PC by using Remote Desktop, your laptop's screen looks just like the computer to which you're connecting.

to which you're connecting. You can run the home computer's programs, move the cursor, manage files and folders, access network data, and even print to network printers!

But you can use Remote Desktop in others ways than accessing a home PC when you're away from home. You can access any PC remotely, as long as it's set up to allow the connection. For instance, you can set up Remote Desktop on a PC in your basement and access that basement computer without having to actually go down to the basement. You can even run a program on another PC if need be. In fact, you can use Remote Desktop to offer assistance to someone who needs help solving a computer problem.

In this chapter, the main focus is on accessing a home PC and home network when you're away from your house. One example of this is to use your laptop from a hotel room to access your own PC and network files.

Know the System and Network Requirements

The only downside of using Remote Desktop, if there is one, is that the computer that receives the remote connection must be running Windows Vista Business, Enterprise, or Ultimate. If you have only Windows Vista Home Premium on your PCs, you'll have to upgrade one of them. However, the computer used to connect, most likely a laptop, can be running almost any Windows operating system at all, including Windows 95, Windows 98, Windows ME, Windows XP, and Windows Vista, among others. You can even connect by using Mac OS X and Linux. (You'll need to visit *www.microsoft.com/downloads* to get the required software for older versions of Windows, though.)

Create a Virtual Private Network

You can connect to a computer on your network by dialing into it or by connecting to it via the Internet. The latter is preferable for many reasons, mostly because dialing is "old school" (slow) and requires that both PCs have a phone line connected to it. When you connect to a remote PC using the Internet, you can connect to your host PC, without the need for a long-distance provider or telephone line, making access more widely available.

One way to connect through the Internet is to connect using a virtual private network (VPN). With a VPN, the host and remote computers can connect to the Internet however they want by using Wi-Fi, broadband, a cable modem, or even dial-up. The downside of VPNs, if there is one, is that the host PC must have a fixed IP address. Your host computer probably doesn't have that. Getting a fixed IP address requires you to contact your ISP and pay a little extra every month for the privilege. VPNs are also extremely secure. Data that travels between the two computers is encrypted, which makes hacking into it virtually impossible. If you want to know more about VPNs and fixed IP addresses, visit *www.microsoft.com*, and search for *virtual private networks*.

If you have a fixed IP address, you can set up the VPN connection the same way you set up the direct connection network in Chapter 3. With VPN, though, you'll choose to connect through the Internet versus any other options. The rest of the setup is easy. Once a VPN is set up, Windows Vista will listen for connection requests.

Set Up the Host PC

The first step in setting up Remote Desktop is to turn on and configure the host PC to accept incoming remote connections. Remember, this PC must be running Windows Vista Business, Enterprise, or Ultimate and be connected to the Internet. The host PC is the one to which you want to connect.

ALLOW REMOTE ACCESS

To turn on and allow remote desktop connections on the host PC, follow these steps:

1. Click Start, Control Panel.
2. Click System And Maintenance.

3. Under System, click Allow Remote Access.

4. Click Continue to proceed.

5. In the System Properties dialog box, shown in Figure 13-1, click the Remote tab, which appears by default.

6. Verify Allow Remote Assistance Connections To This Computer is selected (and select it if it isn't), and under Remote Desktop select Allow Connections From Computers Running Any Version Of Remote Desktop (Less Secure). As shown in Figure 13-1, the default is not to allow connections at all. You have to change that. (If you're confused about Remote Assistance, read the side-bar "Remote Desktop vs. Remote Assistance.")

7. Leave this dialog box open.

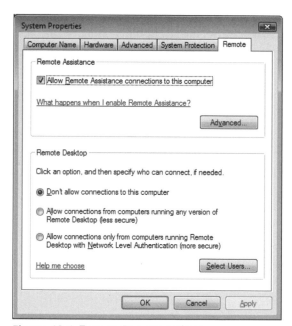

Figure 13-1 Turn on Remote Assistance.

REMOTE DESKTOP VS. REMOTE ASSISTANCE

You might be wondering why I'm talking about Remote Desktop in this chapter, and here you're asked to turn on Remote Assistance. Both tools involve remote access and use the same underlying technologies, so the process for turning them on is the same.

Remote Desktop is used when you want to access your own PC remotely and accessing it requires a username and password. When connected using Remote Desktop, you are the only person who sees your desktop. Other users see the welcome screen on the host and nothing else. That's because you're automatically logged off the host when you connect as the guest remotely.

Remote Assistance is used when a logged-on user wants help from a support technician or IT administrator. The guest logs onto the remote computer only when invited, and both the user and the guest stay logged on at the same time. With Remote Assistance, both users see the same desktop. While Remote Desktop is used to access a host PC for the purpose of accessing one's own files, Remote Assistance is used for the purpose of getting help from a support technician.

Remote Assistance is available with all editions of Windows Vista. Remote Desktop can be set up only on Windows Vista Business, Ultimate, and Enterprise editions, although almost any guest PC can be used.

SELECT USERS

Continuing from the previous steps, you now need to select what users can access the host PC, and thus the network, remotely. To continue the setup, follow these steps:

1. On the Remote tab of the System Properties dialog box, click Select Users.

2. Note who already has access. In Figure 13-2, the user Joli already has access. (Look right above the Add button.) To add another user, click Add. (Note that you can access the user accounts feature from here too, if you need to create a new account.)

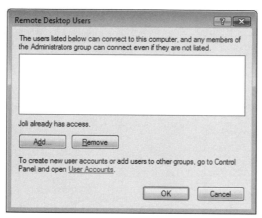

Figure 13-2 Select remote users.

3. In the Select Users dialog box, type the name of the user to add.

4. Click Check Names. If the user name is not recognized, you'll need to add that user in User Accounts. Make sure to create a password for the new user if you create one.

5. Continue to add users as desired, and when finished, click OK.

6. Click OK again to close the Remote Desktop Users dialog box and OK once more to close System Properties.

Make the Connection

Once Remote Desktop is on at the host computer, you can connect to it from another computer. In the following scenario, you'll connect to a computer remotely that is on your own local network, in the same building or home. Later, you'll learn how to connect through a VPN.

WINDOWS FIREWALL AND REMOTE DESKTOP CONNECTIONS

You need to know how to verify whether Windows Firewall will allow Remote Desktop. By default, Windows Firewall does not allow these connections unless you specifically allow them. To verify Windows Firewall is configured correctly, follow these steps:

1. Click Start, Control Panel, and under Security, click Allow A Program Through Windows Firewall.

2. Click Continue.

3. In the Windows Firewall Settings dialog box, scroll down to Remote Assistance. Verify it is selected. If it isn't, select it.

4. Click OK.

CONNECT TO COMPUTER ON THE LOCAL NETWORK

To connect remotely to a computer on your own network, one that is in the basement, upstairs, or even on another floor of an office building, follow these steps:

1. From the guest PC (the one you want to use to connect to the host PC), click Start, All Programs, Accessories, Remote Desktop Connection.

2. In the Remote Desktop Connection window, click Options to expand it. The Remote Desktop Connection window should look like what's shown in Figure 13-3.

3. Type the name of the computer to connect to, and click Connect.

4. Type your user name and password. Click Remember My Credentials if desired. Click OK.

5. If prompted after connecting that another user is currently logged on to the computer, click Yes to prompt the user to disconnect. Figure 13-4 shows the dialog box a logged-on user will see (on the host computer) if you try

to connect remotely to a machine that they are logged on to. Since two people cannot be logged on to the same machine at the same time, the logged-on user must disconnect. If there is no activity in 30 seconds, the user will be disconnected automatically.

Figure 13-3 View all options in the Remote Desktop Connection window.

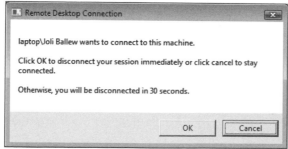

Figure 13-4 Any user logged on to the host computer while you try to connect remotely will be prompted to log off.

6. You will now be able to see the remote computer's screen on your PC. The background screen will be black, and you'll have access to everything installed on the computer, including the network. Figure 13-5 shows an example.

7. To disconnect, click the black X at the top of the screen. When prompted that this action will disconnect your Windows session, click OK.

Figure 13-5 Once connected, the background screen will be black, and you'll have access to the host computer.

NOTE Figure 13-5 shows the client software with which you're accessing the host computer. It's called Tsclient (the Terminal Services client). How Tsclient works is rather technical, but just know that it's the interface through which Remote Desktop works. You don't have to do anything other than the follow the instructions for Remote Desktop in this chapter, and Tsclient will be set up automatically.

CONNECT TO A REMOTE COMPUTER BY USING A VPN

If you're connecting through a VPN, all the steps are the same except for the connection you make prior to logging on to the remote computer. To make the initial connection, follow these steps:

1. Click Start, Network.

2. Open the Network and Sharing Center.

3. In the Tasks pane, click Set Up A Connection Or Network.

4. Select Connect To A Workplace. See Figure 13-6. Click Next.

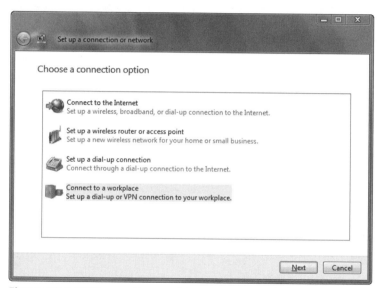

Figure 13-6 VPNs are often used to connect to workplaces.

5. When prompted how to connect, select Use My Internet Connection (VPN).

6. Type the host name or the IP address of the VPN host computer.

7. Click Don't Connect Now; Just Set It Up So I Can Connect Later. Click Next.

8. Type your user name, password, and, if required, a domain name. See Figure 13-7.

9. Click Create.

10. You're now ready to connect. Click Connect Now or Close.

The next time you want to use this connection to connect, click Start, Connect To, and select the VPN connection from the choices. See Figure 13-8.

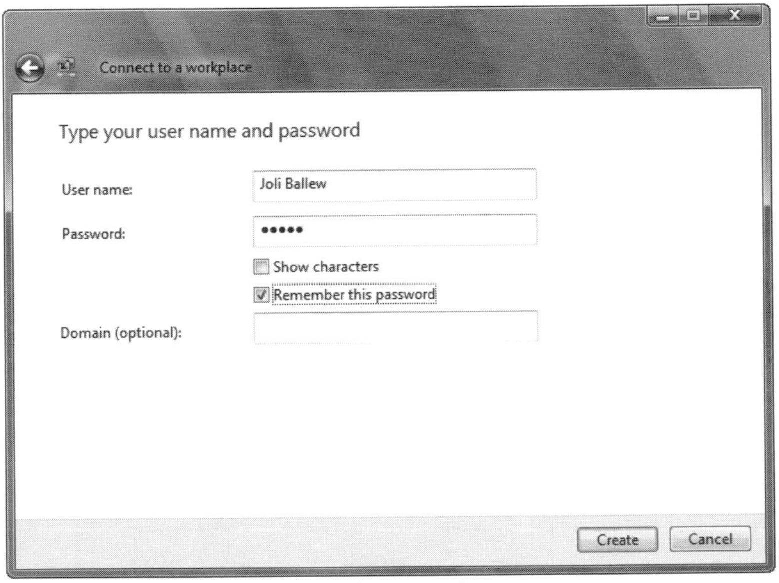

Figure 13-7 Type a user name and password.

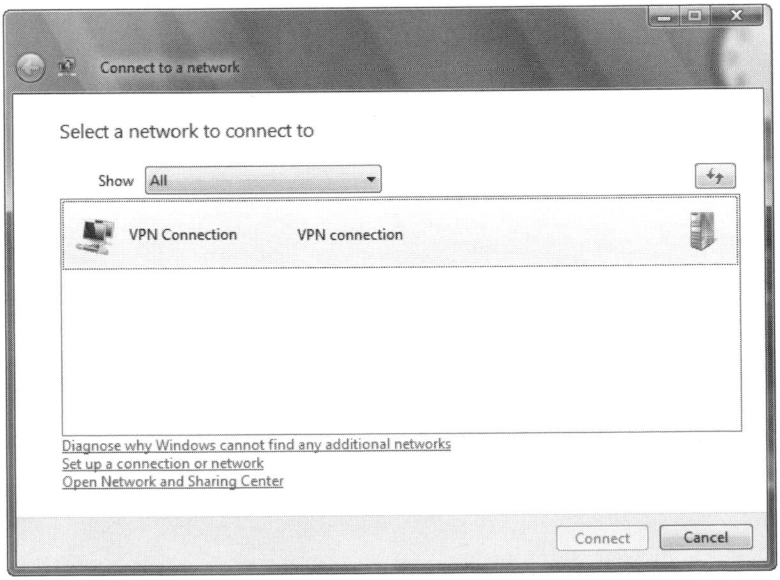

Figure 13-8 Select your VPN connection to connect.

Configure Additional Settings

You probably noticed that the Remote Desktop Connection dialog box offers lots of tabs with all kinds of additional settings to configure. Although you might not ever need to change any of them, it's good to know they're there, just in case. This section will cover all the tabs in the Remote Desktop Connection dialog box, starting with the General tab. Understand that you need to make changes when you are not connected to the remote PC.

GENERAL

On the General tab you can enter the name of the remote computer or browse for the computer to which you want to connect. Browsing is a good idea if you can't remember what the name of the computer is that you want to connect to, provided you're connected to your local network and can browse for it.

You can also select Always Ask For Credentials. You should select this box, especially if you use a laptop. If it gets lost or stolen, it wouldn't take much for someone to access your network if the settings are saved and you automatically log on.

Finally, you can save the connection settings to a file or open any saved connection if desired.

DISPLAY

When you connect to a host PC remotely, you connect by using the default display settings already configured in Remote Desktop. To see these settings, click the Display tab. See Figure 13-9.

The first setting you might want to change is how large the remote desktop size is. The default is to make it as large as possible. You can make the remote desktop size smaller by moving the slider to the left.

You can also change the color settings. Here the setting is at its highest, 32-bit. If you find that the connection is too slow or you notice a performance problem, you can change this to a smaller setting. The less information that must be transmitted, the better!

Finally, Display The Connection Bar When In Full Screen Mode is selected by default. This allows you to easily see the name of the connection you've made and have access to disconnection options on the Desktop. Deselect it if desired.

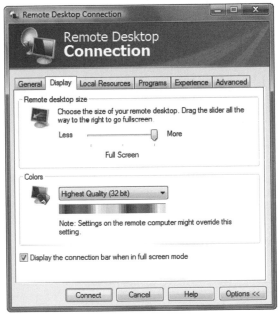

Figure 13-9 Change the default display settings.

LOCAL RESOURCES

You can include local resources and devices in your remote connections. On the Local Resources tab, you can bring the remote computer's sounds to your computer, choose not to play sounds, or leave sounds at the remote computer.

You can include keyboard combinations too. For instance, you can configure this option to apply key combinations only when in full-screen mode, only on the local computer, or only on the remote computer. It's up to you.

Finally, you can select the devices and resources you want to have access to in your remote session, and the options are Printers and Clipboard. Click More to select Smart Cards, Serial Ports, Dries, and Plug And Play Devices.

PROGRAMS

On the Programs tab, you can configure a program to start when the connection is made. You'll have to type the complete path name, so make sure you can locate the program before you add it here! A sample path may look like C:\Program Files\ Internet Explorer\iExplore.

EXPERIENCE

How you experience your remote connection depends on a number of things, such as the desktop background color, menu and window animation, themes, and more. Your experience is also defined by how fast your connection speed is. You can change your connection speed and select what you want to allow through your remote connection from the Experience page. Remember, though, the more information you have to send through the network, the longer it will take to get there. Be careful in what you add. If you notice a performance problem, return here to deselect some of the items.

You can transfer the following from the host to the guest PC:

- Desktop Background
- Font Smoothing
- Desktop Composition
- Contents Of Windows While Dragging
- Menus And Window Animations
- Themes
- Bitmap Caching

You can also tell Windows that you want to reconnect if the connection is dropped. Figure 13-10 shows how you might configure your connection.

Figure 13-10 The Experience tab.

ADVANCED

You probably won't need to do much here, because the default settings are usually the best. However, you have a couple of choices:

- Server Authentication
- Connect From Anywhere

SERVER AUTHENTICATION

Authentication verifies that you are connecting to the correct remote computer. This keeps you from connecting to the wrong computer (although this is likely not an issue on your network). There are three options:

Always Connect, Even If Authentication Fails (Least Secure) With this option, you'll be connected even if verification and authentication fails.

Warn Me If Authentication Fails (More Secure) With this option, you get to choose whether you want to connect if verification or authentication fails.

Do No Connect If Authentication Fails (Most Secure) With this option, if Remote Desktop Connection cannot verify the identity of the remote computer, you won't be able to connect.

Note that remote computers running Windows Server 2003 Service Pack 1 or earlier cannot provide their identity for verification. If your remote computer is running this type of operating system, select Always Connect, Even If Authentication Fails.

CONNECT FROM ANYWHERE

These settings are for connecting to a remote computer when a Terminal Services gateway server is required. If you don't know what that is, keep the default, Automatically Detect TS Gateway Server Settings. If you know what a Terminal Services gateway server and you use one, ask your administrator for the settings you should use. You'll likely select Use These TS Gateway Server Settings, and you'll type your server name and select a logon method.

Chapter Summary

In this chapter, you learned how to set up a Remote Desktop connection. You learned about meeting minimum requirements including have Windows Vista Business, Enterprise, or Ultimate installed on the host PC. You learned how to set up a host PC, a VPN, and a guest computer. You learned how to make the connection and how to configure additional and optional settings.

CHAPTER 14

Maintain a Healthy Network

- **Work with Windows Security Center**
- **Guard against security threats**
- **Configure User Account Control**
- **Work with Windows Update**
- **Work with Windows Defender**
- **Work with Windows Firewall**
- **Work with Windows Backup and Restore**
- **Take care of your hardware**

ONCE YOUR NETWORK is up and running, it's up to you to keep it healthy. This means incorporating all of the security features that come with the Windows Vista operating system and taking care of your network hardware properly. If your network computers aren't healthy, your network isn't healthy either. Remember, a chain is only as strong as its weakest link!

*If your network com-
puters aren't healthy,
your network isn't
healthy either.*

In this chapter, you'll learn how to use, include, and configure Windows Security Center, Windows Update, Windows Defender, Windows Firewall, and Windows Backup and Restore, as well as how to properly take care of your network hardware.

Use Windows Security Center

You'll find the Windows Security Center in Control Panel's Security section. Using the Security Center, you can perform lots of tasks:

- You can look for updates.

- You can verify the computer's security status.

- You can turn on or off automatic updating.

- You can verify the firewall status.

- You can require a password when the computer wakes.

Figure 14-1 shows an example of the Security Center. Notice that two "security essentials" are not being met. One of these is malware protection; the other consists of settings configured specifically for this PC. In Figure 14-1, both Malware Protection and Other Security Settings are expanded to show the problems associated with this particular computer.

To see how your computer ranks with Security Center, follow these steps:

1. Click Start, and click Control Panel.

2. Click Security.

3. Click Security Center.

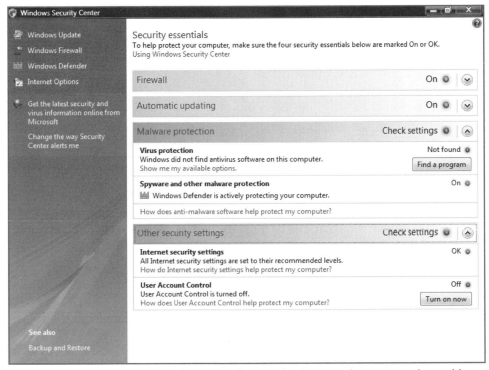

Figure 14-1 The Security Essentials page in the Security Center points out security problems.

RESOLVE SECURITY ESSENTIALS ISSUES

If everything is on and all lights are green on the Security Essentials page, move to other Windows-based PCs on your network. Make sure to examine all the PCs for security holes. If you can't find any problems, you can skip this part of the chapter. However, if any of the items in the list are not on and you see the Check Settings notice, read on. Your PC has security issues.

> **TIP** Make sure to open the Security Center on all your Windows Vista–based PCs and verify the security status of each. Additionally, write down every problem, and make sure the other PCs on your network, servers, and Windows XP–based PCs do not have similar issues.

FIREWALL

Unless you have a third-party firewall installed, you should have Windows Firewall turned on. A firewall protects your computer by looking at what comes into your network, and it blocks dangerous software. You'll learn much more about firewalls in the section "Use Windows Firewall" later in this chapter.

AUTOMATIC UPDATING

Updates are software that need to be installed on your computer. These updates include fixes for security holes, among other things. Automatic updating should be turned on. You'll learn much more about updates in the section "Use Windows Update" later in this chapter.

MALWARE PROTECTION

You should have some sort of virus protection installed on every computer. Additionally, anti-malware protection is now necessary too. This kind of protection has lots of options, and you'll learn more about your options in the section "Protect Your Computer from Viruses" later in this chapter.

OTHER SECURITY SETTINGS

You may also see the Check Settings notification under Other Security Settings. Expand this section to see what security issues Windows has found. Security problems can be caused by Internet security settings, User Account Control settings, and more. You'll learn more about User Account Control later in the section "Turn On User Account Controls."

EXPLORE THE SECURITY CENTER TASKS PANE

In the Windows Security Tasks pane, you'll see quick links to the following:

- Windows Update
- Windows Firewall
- Windows Defender
- Internet Options
- Get The Latest Security And Virus Information Online From Microsoft
- Change The Way Security Center Alerts Me

Almost all of these items have their own section in this chapter, except for the last three in this list. You'll look at these here.

SET INTERNET OPTIONS

Clicking Internet Options in the Security Center opens the Internet Properties dialog box to the Security tab, shown in Figure 14-2. By default, Internet is selected. The default settings for Internet security are appropriate for most networks.

Figure 14-2 The Internet Properties dialog box lets you configure Internet security settings.

The Internet setting is Medium by default, which prompts you before download-ing potentially unsafe content, and it will not download ActiveX controls. It is not important to know what these things are, but it is important to be protected from them. You can change the security level by moving the slider up, and you might want to try Medium-High to further protect your computer.

The Local Intranet setting is Medium-Low by default, which is generally appropri-ate for local networks. Most content will not be run without a prompt, unsigned

ActiveX controls will not be downloaded, and this setting includes all the Medium-level restrictions as well.

As long as you incorporate Windows Firewall, Windows Update, Windows Defender, and User Account Control and have installed antivirus software, you don't need to change these settings.

GET THE LATEST SECURITY AND VIRUS INFORMATION

Clicking Get The Latest Security And Virus Information Online From Microsoft in the Tasks pane opens the Microsoft Security Web site. Here you can read top stories related to the latest security tools and threats and articles written by security specialists to help you further secure your PC and network. You can also download and install the free Malicious Software Removal Tool, a lifesaver if you have already acquired malicious software on your PC.

CHANGE THE SECURITY ALERT SETTINGS

Clicking Change The Way Security Center Alerts Me in the Security Center's Tasks pane opens the dialog box shown in Figure 14-3. You have three choices for how the Security Center will alert you when your computer might be at risk.

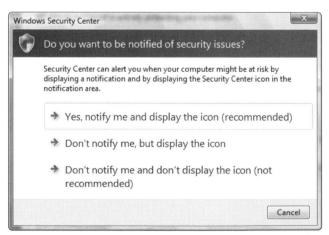

Figure 14-3 You can change how the Security Center notifies you of security issues.

Protect Your Computer from Viruses

Microsoft recommends you install security software to help protect your computer from viruses and other security issues and that you keep the software up to date. Lots of companies offer this type of protection:

- Symantec at *www.symantecstore.com*
- AVG at *www5.grisoft.com*
- CA at *http://home3.ca.com/Microsoft*
- Kaspersky at *www.kaspersky.com/vista*
- Trend Micro at *www.trendmicro.com*

You can also choose Windows Live OneCare. The home page is at *http://onecare.live.com*, and there's currently a 90-day free trial. Windows Live OneCare has everything you need to protect your PC, including the following:

- Antivirus
- Antispyware
- Antiphishing
- Firewall
- Performance tune-ups
- Backup and restore capabilities

If you are in need of security protection, this may be the best way to go. From the Windows Live OneCare Web site, you can add computers to your subscription, download the product, read about top security threats, and even visit the Windows Live OneCare team blog. Whatever type of protection you choose is up to you; just make sure you get protection!

WHEN TO SUSPECT A VIRUS OR SPYWARE

You might have malicious code on your computer if you see any of the following:

- New toolbars, links, or favorites you did not add yourself.
- Your home page has been changed (hijacked).
- Your pointer changes.
- Your search engine changes.
- You see pop-up ads even when you aren't connected to the Internet.
- You can't visit Web sites you want to visit (you're taken to another site).
- Your computer is slower than usual.

Work with User Account Control

User Account Control (UAC) is a security feature included with Windows Vista that helps prevent unauthorized changes to your computer. It works by asking you for an administrator name and password or requiring you to click Continue (depending on what type of account you're logged on with) before any action is taken that could potentially damage your computer or cause system-wide changes. This applies to all users, even your children and co-workers. With UAC turned on, no one can install software or otherwise change system settings without administrator credentials. Administrators must click Continue to move forward. This helps control unauthorized access by malicious software programs you might acquire on the Internet.

RESOLVE FOUR TYPES OF UAC MESSAGES

When UAC is on, you'll be prompted with four types of UAC messages. To resolve each, you either need to type an administrator name and password or, if already logged on as an administrator, click Continue. The four messages are detailed next:

Windows Needs Your Permission To Continue A Windows function or program that can affect other users of this computer needs your permission to start. Look at the name of the action or program to verify you know what it is, and whether it is a program or function you want to run, type your administrator credentials, or click Continue.

A Program Needs Your Permission To Continue A program that's not part of Windows needs your permission to start. This particular program has a valid digital signature (you'll be prompted if it does not) and thus helps ensure the program is compatible with Windows Vista and is from a recognized publisher. If you want to run this program, type your administrator credentials, or click Continue.

An Unidentified Program Wants To Access Your Computer An unidentified program that does not have a valid digital signature is trying to gain access to the computer. The program may not be what it seems to be, and you may not want to install it. If you are sure you trust the publisher of the software, type your administrator credentials, or click Continue.

This Program Has Been Blocked This message indicates the program has been blocked by the administrator of the computer and cannot be run without the administrator unblocking it.

TURN ON OR OFF USER ACCOUNT CONTROL

UAC is turned on by default. It is best to leave it turned on. However, if you must turn it off or verify it's turned on, work through the following steps:

1. Click Start, and click Control Panel.

2. Click User Accounts And Family Safety.

3. Click User Accounts.

4. Click Turn User Account Control On Or Off.

5. Select Use User Account Control (UAC) To Help Protect Your Computer to turn on UAC, or deselect it to turn it off. See Figure 14-4.

Figure 14-4 Turn on UAC for better security.

Use Windows Update

Windows Update is available in Control Panel's Security section. *Updates* are software patches to the operating system, the Microsoft Office system, and even the drivers installed on your computer. Some updates are critical, meaning they need to be installed for the computer to run properly and to remain secure. Some updates are options and do not have to be installed if you don't want to install them. (Of course, you can turn off Windows Update completely, but that is not recommended.)

VERIFY OR CHANGE WINDOWS UPDATE SETTINGS

When Windows Update is on, which it is by default, you get to choose how you want updates to be downloaded and installed. Figure 14-5 shows the Windows Update options.

To access this page and make changes to Windows Update settings, follow these steps:

1. Click Start, click Control Panel, and click Security.

2. Under Windows Update, select Turn Automatic Updating On Or Off.

3. Select how you want Windows to get updates. The choices include the following:

- Install Updates Automatically (Recommended)
- Download Updates But Let Me Choose Whether To Install Them
- Check For Updates But Let Me Choose Whether To Download And Install Them
- Never Check For Updates (Not Recommended)

NOTE For Install Updates Automatically (Recommended), select the times to obtain the updates.

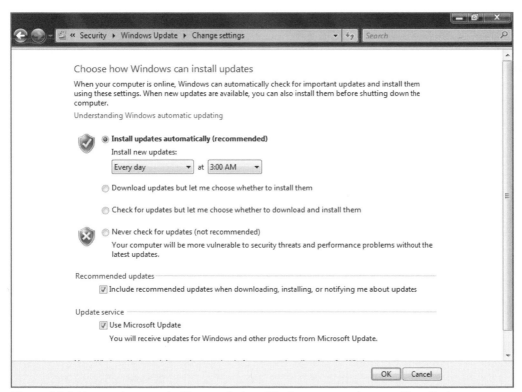

Figure 14-5 You are in control of how and when Windows gets updates and installs them.

4. Decide whether to include recommended updates. Recommended updates are, well, recommended, but they are not critical updates.

5. Decide whether to use Microsoft Update. This service sends updates for Windows and other products to you.

OBTAIN AND INSTALL WINDOWS UPDATES MANUALLY

You can look for downloaded updates anytime or get the updates manually. You can do this in several ways, but the fastest is probably to click Start, All Programs, Windows Update. In the Windows Update window, you may see updates that have already been downloaded but not installed, as shown in Figure 14-6. Also notice in the Tasks pane are links to look for updates, change settings, view update history, and restore hidden updates.

To look for updates manually, click Check For Updates. If any updates are available, you'll be informed. The results will look like what's shown in Figure 14-6. You can now install the updates or view the available updates and select only the ones you want. Clicking View Optional Updates opens a window like the one shown in Figure 14-7. You select the updates to install. Once selected, click Install.

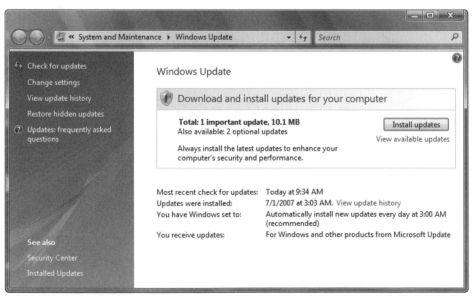

Figure 14-6 The Windows Update window offers downloaded updates and a link to look for updates manually.

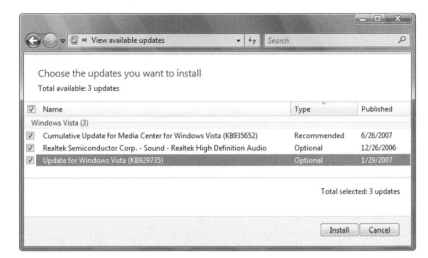

Figure 14-7 You get to choose what updates to install.

TIP Windows Vista will create a System Restore point prior to installation, so if for some reason something goes wrong with the update, you can return to the pre-update condition.

Figure 14-8 shows an installation in progress. Notice that your Windows Update settings are also summarized.

Figure 14-8 Installing updates is automatic.

Use Windows Defender

Although third-party antivirus software is recommended, Windows Vista does come with some antivirus protection, Windows Defender. Windows Defender offers three tools to help keep your computer virus, spyware, and malware free: built-in, automatic, real-time protection from online threats; an online community in which you can participate called Microsoft SpyNet; and options for scanning your computer for malicious code and removing any that is found. You can also open Windows Defender anytime you want to see whether your computer is infected, to scan the computer, and to see whether your computer is running normally. When you open Windows Defender, you want to see what shown in Figure 14-9.

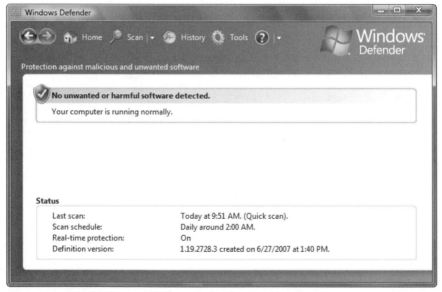

Figure 14-9 In this figure, Windows Defender does not detect any unwanted or harmful software.

GET REAL-TIME PROTECTION

As noted, Windows Defender offers real-time protection from online threats. This means you'll be alerted immediately when potentially unwanted software attempts to install itself on your computer. You can choose to ignore, quarantine, remove, or allow the threat that is found.

SCAN FOR SPYWARE

You can perform two basic types of scans with Windows Defender: a quick scan and a full scan. If you think your computer is infected, you can also create a custom scan.

A *quick scan* looks in the places where malicious code is usually found. By default, quick scans are performed once a day. You can perform a quick scan anytime you want from Windows Defender.

A *full scan* scans every part of your computer and takes much longer than a quick scan. You should perform a full scan once a month, preferably at night or when you aren't using the computer.

A *custom scan* lets you decide what part of the computer to scan. You select the drives and folders. This is a good option if you need to scan a CD, DVD, file, or something stored on a removable drive.

REMOVE MALICIOUS CODE

If spyware or other malicious code is found on your computer, you can remove it. When Windows Defender finds this software, it alerts you. As noted previously, your options include removing the infected program.

Unfortunately, Windows Defender doesn't catch everything. That's why you need a dedicated antivirus program. If a virus does make its way onto your computer, you'll probably use the third-party software to uninstall it. Follow the manufacturer's instructions for doing so.

JOIN THE MICROSOFT SPYWARE COMMUNITY

You can join the Microsoft Spyware community from the Tools option in Windows Defender. To see this option and other tools, follow these steps:

1. Click Start, click Control Panel, click Security, and click Windows Defender.

2. From the Windows Defender toolbar, shown in Figure 14-10, click Tools.

3. Click Microsoft SpyNet.

4. On the Join Microsoft SpyNet page, select Join With A Basic Membership. Later, you can join with an advanced membership if you enjoy the community.

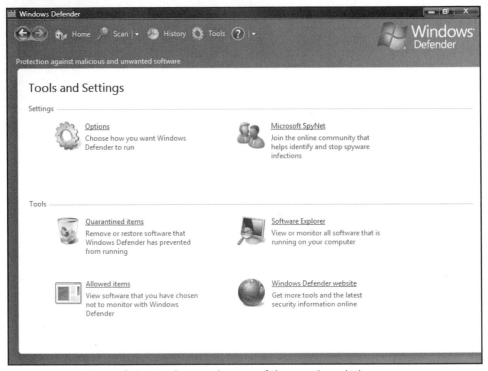

Figure 14-10 Microsoft SpyNet lets you be part of the security solution.

CHANGE WINDOWS DEFENDER SETTINGS

You can also change your Windows Defender settings from the Tools options. The changes you can make include but are not limited to the following:

- Changing how often and at what times scans are performed

- Configuring default actions for alert items for security threats

- Deciding whether to use Windows Defender

- Selecting the Windows security agents you want to run (including Internet Explorer add-ons, Windows add-ons, and system configuration settings)

- Deciding to scan archived files and folders

- Deciding to create System Restore points prior to applying actions to detected threats

Use Windows Firewall

You can find the Windows Firewall options and settings where you have found all the other security features included so far in this chapter—from Start, Control Panel, Security. Windows Firewall is an option in the Security window.

A firewall is a software or a hardware solution for keeping your computer safe by unwanted data from passing through your network. A firewall looks at what comes in from the Internet, and if it's deemed malicious or unwanted, it blocks the data from entering. By default, Windows Firewall is on.

CONFIGURE GENERAL WINDOWS FIREWALL SETTINGS

Windows Firewall offers quite a few settings to help you personalize how you want the firewall to work. You can find basic settings on the Windows Firewall Settings dialog box's General tab, shown in Figure 14-11.

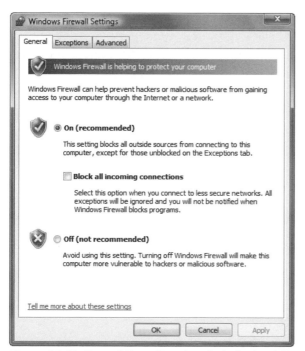

Figure 14-11 General firewall settings include the ability to turn on or off the firewall.

It's best to leave the firewall settings on. The On (Recommended) setting blocks unwanted data from the Internet from attacking your network. You can create exceptions, though, using the Exceptions tab. There is more on this shortly.

You can also choose to block all connections. Blocking all connections should be used only when you connect to a network that is not a secure network. All exceptions will be ignored, as well as all incoming requests to connect to your PC or network.

The last option is to turn Windows Firewall off. This is not recommended unless you've installed a third-party firewall solution. The solution can be hardware or software based. If you are using a second firewall solution, it's best to turn off Windows Firewall. Multiple firewalls can cause problems for networks and connectivity.

CONFIGURE FIREWALL EXCEPTIONS

An exception configured in a firewall allows the program or port associated with the exception to move through the firewall unhindered. Figure 14-12 shows the Windows Firewall Settings dialog box's Exceptions tab. You'll notice that some exceptions are configured already. Exceptions are automatically configured when you choose to allow a program when prompted by UAC, and you can create exceptions manually by selecting the boxes shown here.

Figure 14-12 Exceptions let programs move through the firewall unhindered.

You may never need to manually create an exception, since exceptions will automatically be created when you choose to allow a port or program by inputting administrator credentials when prompted by UAC, but it doesn't hurt to know that option is available. Looking at the Program Or Port list, you should see several programs you recognize and specifically allowed yourself:

- File and printer sharing
- Windows Media Center extenders
- Network discovery
- Remote assistance
- Windows Home Server Connector

UNDERSTAND ADVANCED FIREWALL OPTIONS

The Windows Firewall Settings dialog box's Advanced tab offers options to configure network connection settings for each of your network connections. This may include a dial-up connection, a local area connection, or even a VPN connection. By default, when Windows Firewall is turned on, all connections are selected for protection. You can deselect a connection if desired, although I don't recommend this. You can also restore the defaults for Windows Firewall, if desired.

Use Windows Backup and Restore Center

The Windows Backup and Restore Center lets you create and configure automatic backups of the data on your computer. If you don't have a Windows Home Server PC, this is a good backup strategy.

The Windows Backup and Restore Center, once set up, will remember to perform the backups for you, and that's good. You've probably forgotten or simply put off creating a backup yourself. Maybe you've even lost data. With a strategy in place to have backups automatically created, you can save yourself quite a bit of heartbreak if something ever happens to your PC.

BACK UP DATA FUNDAMENTALS

The Backup and Restore Center is located in Control Panel; just click the System And Maintenance option, and then click Backup And Restore Center. Clicking Back Up Files, shown in Figure 14-13, opens the application, shown in Figure 14-14.

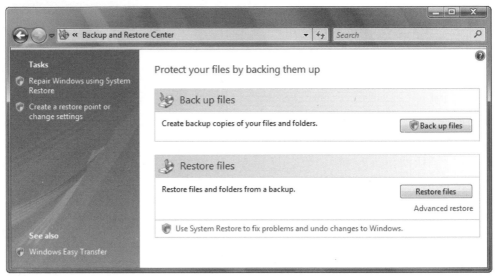

Figure 14-13 The Backup and Restore Center offers Back Up Files and Restore Files options, among others.

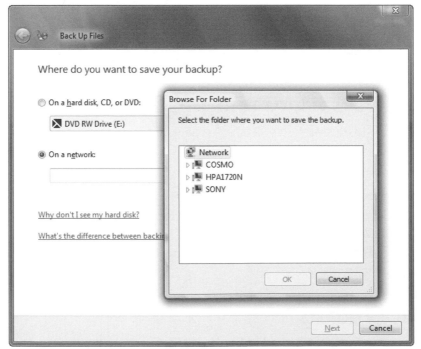

Figure 14-14 The first step of backing up files is to choose a place to store the backup.

You really need to be concerned with only two types of backups at this time. They include your personal data and the computer's system data.

PERSONAL DATA

Personal data includes but is not limited to the files and folders you create and modify and the data you obtain elsewhere such as music you download from the Internet. You should configure the Backup and Restore Center to back up your personal data at least once a week. You should also perform a manual backup prior to making changes to your PC, such as adding a new piece of hardware or software.

SYSTEM DATA AND PC IMAGES

> **TIP** This section applies only to those with Windows Vista Ultimate, configured with an NTFS files system. If you don't Windows Vista Ultimate, skip to the next section. If you do, read on!

A computer has data that applies only to itself. This includes things such as registry entries, hardware device drivers, system settings, programs you've installed, and data the operating system needs to run. If something happens to your computer, without the proper backup, you'd lose this information. If you have Windows Vista Ultimate, you can create a backup just for this type of data, though. It's called a Complete PC Backup Image, because it backs up all this along with your personal data. If you need to, you can use this backup to restore your PC if you have a system-wide failure.

You don't get to choose what gets restored and what doesn't with this type of backup, though, which makes this an all-or-nothing recovery option based on whatever your last complete backup includes. If you have Windows Vista Ultimate, you should create this type of backup twice a year. Doing so always gives you a going-back point, if for some reason you can't restore using other means. You also need to make sure you back up all the partitions on your PCs.

WINDOWS VISTA ULTIMATE, SYSTEM IMAGES, AND NTFS

A file system keeps data on a hard disk organized. FAT32 is one option, and NTFS is another. NTFS is preferred because it offers the ability to recover automatically from disk errors, supports large disks, and offers better security by allowing NTFS permissions and encryption to be placed on files and folders.

Most likely your Windows Vista Ultimate PC is configured with NTFS. If it isn't and you don't dual boot with an older operating system such as Windows 98, you should convert the hard disk to NTFS. To make the conversion, follow these steps:

1. Click Start, click All Programs, click Accessories, and click Command Prompt.

2. Right-click Command Prompt, and select Run As Administrator.

3. Click Continue.

4. At the command prompt, type the following: **convert e: /fs:ntfs**. Here, e: is the drive letter; replace this letter with the drive to convert.

5. Type the name of the hard drive or partition. You can find the name of the volume by clicking Start and then clicking Computer. The Computer window will open that contains information about all the drives installed on the PC.

BACK UP TO A NETWORK DRIVE

To back up personal files on your computer to a network drive, possibly an external drive or another computer, follow these steps:

1. Click Start, click Control Panel, click System and Maintenance, and click Backup And Restore Center.

2. Click Backup Files.

3. Click Continue to begin.

4. On the Where Do You Want To Save Your Backup? page, select On A Network. Click Browse. The Browse For Folder dialog box opens, as shown in Figure 14-15.

5. Expand the network computer, and locate where you'd like to save the backup. Once you've selected the folder or drive, click OK. Click Next.

6. If prompted, type a user name and password, and click OK.

7. If prompted regarding what disks to back up, select the disks, and click Next.

Figure 14-15 You choose where to save the backup.

8. On the Which File Types Do You Want To Back Up? page, select all the file types. Note that you can deselect file types, but it's best not to do so. Click Next.

9. Select how often you want to create a backup. Choices include the following:

   How often Select Daily, Weekly, Monthly.

   What day Select from a weekday or a day of the month. No choice is offered if you select Daily.

   What time Make sure the computer will be on during this time.

10. Select Save Settings and Start Backup.

RESTORE WITH WINDOWS BACKUP AND RESTORE CENTER

To recover personal files using a backup, open the Backup and Restore Center, and click Restore. A wizard will walk you through the process. You'll need to make sure the network drive where you saved the backup is available so the backup can be accessed.

TRY REBOOTING, SYSTEM RESTORE, AND A REPAIR INSTALLATION FIRST

If something goes wrong with your PC, understand that you don't have to use the Backup and Restore Center every time to fix it. System Restore is often enough to resolve the problem, and simply rebooting may fix the issue as well. System Restore is included with all editions of Windows Vista, is on by default, and automatically creates its own restore points each day.

If System Restore doesn't work, you can also perform a repair installation using your Windows Vista disc. Choose the upgrade installation option. You won't lose any data, and this often restores files that are corrupt and gets the operating system working again. Try these two options before using a backup to restore your computer to an earlier time.

Take Care of Your Hardware

You don't just need to take care of your network PCs by securing them with software such as firewalls and antivirus programs; you also need to take care of the hardware that connects them to each other. The computers themselves need a little TLC too; every once in a while you should use canned air to blow dust from the PC's tower and verify there's enough airflow getting to it. There are other things to keep up with too. In the following sections, you'll learn what you need to do to keep the hardware on your network healthy.

THINGS TO LOOK FOR DAILY

You need to keep an eye on a few things every day. Keep in mind that dust, pet hair, and smoke can damage the inside of your PC, and thus keeping these things away from a tower every day is just as important as keeping a proper backup. Here are some other things to watch out for daily:

- Keep pets off your PC's towers and laptop keyboards.
- Avoid smoking around computer equipment.

- Look for frayed wires and cables, including power cords.

- Make sure surge protectors are working.

- Make sure a cable is not caught under a desk or chair.

- Make sure all PC towers are getting adequate air flow.

- Avoid constant shutdowns and reboots. (Configure power settings to put the computer to sleep instead.)

THINGS TO VERIFY MONTHLY

You need to verify and perform some tasks each month, including but not limited to the following:

- Physically clean the PC, especially where dust collects in the back of the tower.

- Make sure connections work, including peripheral connections and Ethernet connections.

- Verify backups are being performed and your backup hardware is properly installed.

- Verify PC towers are on a firm surface and are not being jostled or run into.

- Keep up on the latest virus threats to avoid a potential security issue.

THINGS TO VERIFY BIANNUALLY

You need to do a few tasks a couple of times a year:

- Use canned air to blow dust out of each PC's tower.

- Clean underneath keyboard keys that stick.

- Clean roller-ball mice.

- Verify peripheral cables and Ethernet cables are not being stretched or pinched.

- Verify that wireless access points are optimally placed.

- Make sure power outlets have not become overloaded.

- Defragment your hard drive.

- Make sure your wireless access point is not near any potential interference (such as wireless phone or microwave oven).

- Use Windows Backup and Restore to test your physical backup device.

Chapter Summary

In this chapter, you learned how to keep your network healthy. This includes configuring and managing Windows Update, User Account Control, Windows Defender, Windows Firewall, Windows Backup and Restore, and more. You also learned how to keep hardware from harm, including occasionally using canned air to clean the inside of the PC's tower, monitoring backup devices, and making sure cables and power cords are in good working order.

PART V

Appendix and Glossary

Troubleshoot a Network

- **Use the Network and Sharing Center's diagnostics tools**
- **Verify hardware connections**
- **Explore the Help and Support Center**
- **Ask for remote assistance**
- **Visit Windows Help online**
- **Search the Microsoft Knowledge Base**
- **Post and search in Windows communities**
- **Contact Microsoft Customer Support**

THERE ARE lots of ways to troubleshoot network problems. They range from finding simple fixes using the Network and Sharing Center to contacting Microsoft Customer Support and paying for help. Here, you'll learn a lot of the available help options, including getting help from the Help and Support Center on your PC, asking for remote assistance from a friend, getting help online, searching the Microsoft Knowledge Base, and even posting and searching in Windows communities.

There are lots of ways to troubleshoot network problems.

TIP Always reboot the computer before doing anything else. Oftentimes, rebooting solves the problem.

Use the Network and Sharing Center

The first step in troubleshooting network access is to query the Network and Sharing Center. To access the Network and Sharing Center, click Start, Network. In the Network window, click Network And Sharing Center. In the Tasks pane, click Diagnose And Repair. Wait while the diagnostics complete. See Figure A-1.

Figure A-1 Windows Network Diagnostics tries to find a networking problem.

As shown in Figure A-2, this sometimes works. As shown here, the networking problem is most likely because an Ethernet cable is disconnected or because wireless connectivity is turned off. As noted, to solve the problem, reconnect the cable, or turn on wireless capability.

If the Diagnose And Repair task finds a problem, most of the time the problem can be solved without further troubleshooting. If the problem cannot be solved here, continue troubleshooting.

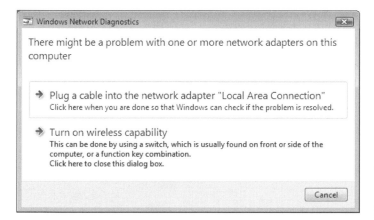

Figure A-2 Once you think you've fixed the problem, use this dialog box to see whether you've really fixed it.

Verify Connections and Reboot

You should always verify the physical connections and reboot the hardware before going continuing with more extensive troubleshooting. Verifying physical connections includes but is not limited to the following:

- Looking for and replacing frayed wires and cables
- Making sure Ethernet connections click into place on hubs, switches, routers, and NICs
- Verifying wireless cards are properly inserted
- Moving wireless access points to a more central location
- Making sure a cable is not pinched or damaged
- Making sure a cable is not caught under a desk or chair
- Verifying NICs are security seated inside the PC tower
- Verifying plugs are inserted into working electrical outlets

To verify some of these items, you may need to swap out an older Ethernet cable for a newer one to verify that the cable itself is not part of the problem. You may also need to plug a lamp into a socket to verify an electrical outlet is working.

Once you've verified the hardware, be sure to reboot the network in the proper order.

POWER CYCLE THE CABLE MODEM

Unplug the power cord to the modem. If the modem has a battery backup that does not allow it to be turned off, take out the battery. After a minute or so, plug it back in, and reinsert the battery if applicable. The cable modem will boot and run through myriad self-tests. After it's fully rebooted (usually between 30 seconds and 2 minutes after restoring power), continue.

POWER CYCLE THE ROUTER

Turn on the hub, switch, or router by plugging it back in and turning it on if necessary. Wait for another few minutes to make sure the router has completed rebooted.

TURN ON THE PCS

Restart the PCs that are connected to the router.

Explore the Help and Support Center

The Windows Help and Support Center offers a special Troubleshooting section just for networking. To access these help pages, click Start, and click Help And Support. Click the Troubleshooting icon, and in the results, locate Networking. The most common network problems are listed, including finding a wireless network, finding computers on a home network, and resolving Internet connection problems.

TROUBLESHOOTING WIRELESS NETWORKS

The Help and Support Center articles are very thorough. For instance, here are just a few of the issues that could make a wireless network unavailable, and the solutions to each are detailed in the Help and Support Center:

- Wireless is not turned on at the PC.
- The PC is too far from the access point.
- The access point is turned off or not working properly.
- Other devices are causing interference.

- Windows is not configured with the right type of network.

- The router or access point is busy.

- The network is not set to broadcast its network name (SSID).

- The network administrator is blocking access to the network.

- The wireless network adapter is in monitor mode.

If you have a wireless network and have just become unable to access it, most likely it is one of these issues.

TROUBLESHOOTING WIRED NETWORKS

As with wireless networks, there is a lot of information in the Help and Support Center for resolving wired network problems. If you can't see computers on your home network, click Start, Network. If you can't access a network computer's shared files, verify the following:

- You need to reconnect (or connect) to the network.

- The computer you want is not connected to the network.

- The workgroup name is incorrect.

- Network discovery has been turned off.

- Network cables have been disconnected.

- The modem, hub, switch, or router has been turned off.

- Power management settings are disconnecting the PC from the network.

TROUBLESHOOT INTERNET CONNECTIONS

Internet connections are often interrupted or fail because of a malfunction in the modem, which needs to be reset. Information about how to reset the modem comes with the hardware itself. Usually, there's a button on the bottom that you can press with a paper clip or pushpin. Cable modems can also have a standby button, which, when turned on, can cause connectivity problems too. Before getting too involved in troubleshooting Internet problems, verify the modem is working, and reboot all hardware. Other problems may include the following:

- The Ethernet cable from the modem to the hub, switch, router, or PC has become disconnected.
- There's an Internet failure at the ISP.
- The DSL filter has become unstable or is not connected.
- The lights on the modem are indicating a modem failure.

And for dial-up, here are some common issues:

- You misdialed the phone number.
- Your phone jack is not working.
- You have incorrectly connected the modem.
- Call waiting is interfering.
- There was an automatic disconnection because of idle time.
- Someone picked up the phone in another room.
- You have a virus or spyware.

Ask for Remote Assistance

You can also ask an online friend for assistance. Windows Remote Assistance is a good way to solve a problem if you have a friend you trust who you think can solve your problem. When you ask for help using Remote Assistance, you will let your friend (or technical support person) connect to your PC. Then, either they can walk you through the problem or you can hand over control of your PC to them and let them solve the problem. Remote Assistance was introduced in Chapter 13, when compared to Remote Desktop. Both Remote Assistance and Remote Desktop use the same underlying remote technologies.

> **TIP** Remote Assistance is a good thing to set up if you are generally the one people come to for help. For instance, if your mom, who lives in another state, needs help often, you can give her Remote Assistance over the Internet.

STARTING REMOTE ASSISTANCE

When you open Windows Help and Support, the first page offers the option to use Windows Remote Assistance to get help from a friend or to offer it. Clicking the Windows Remote Assistance link opens the Windows Remote Assistance dialog box shown in Figure A-3. Depending on your circumstance, you'll either invite someone you trust to help you or offer to help someone.

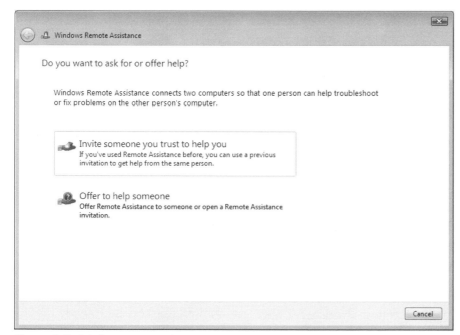

Figure A-3 Ask for remote assistance.

To ask for some remote assistance, click Invite Someone You Trust To Help You. You'll be prompted to choose a method to ask for help, which is best done through e-mail.

CHOOSE A PASSWORD

To secure the connection, you must create and then relay a password to the person from whom you are asking for help. You should do this by phone or in person. Although you can send a separate e-mail, this somewhat defeats the purpose of keeping this transaction secure.

SEND THE E-MAIL

With the password created, the e-mail will be sent automatically. If you chose to create a file, then you should save the file, compose an e-mail yourself, and attach the invitation file. Once the e-mail or file has been sent, the Windows Vista operating system will wait for the incoming connection. This is shown in Figure A-4.

Figure A-4 Windows Vista waits for the incoming connection.

INVITATION ACCEPTANCE

Once your e-mail has been sent, you must wait for the recipient to receive it, open it, and type the password. You'll be prompted to let the user connect. See Figure A-5. Once connected, you and the user can chat using the included instant messaging option, and you can let the user take control of your PC, if you want, and they can work to solve your problem.

Figure A-5 You'll be prompted to let the user connect.

Visit Windows Help Online

You can always visit *http://support.microsoft.com* to search for solutions to your problems. There you'll find the top solution centers you'll need, including one for Windows Vista. The Windows Vista Solution Center currently offers the following categories:

- Error Messages
- Installing and Upgrading
- Using Windows Vista
- Hardware
- Configuring and Maintaining
- Networking
- Entertainment
- Mobile PCs and Devices
- Security and Privacy
- Contact

You'll want to visit Networking. In the Networking section you can browse common networking problems and their solutions. Common problems and solutions include the following:

- Setting up a home network
- Troubleshooting network and Internet connection problems
- Troubleshooting finding wireless networks
- Troubleshooting dial-up connections
- Troubleshooting VPN connections

You can also search the Support and Help content, visit the Windows Vista community, create support page favorites, and more.

Search the Microsoft Knowledge Base

The Microsoft Knowledge Base puts you in control of finding your own solutions. You get to narrow your search by product and specific words. For instance, as shown in Figure A-6, you can search Windows Vista Home Premium for problems related to networking with Windows XP–based PCs. The results offer 155 problems and solutions.

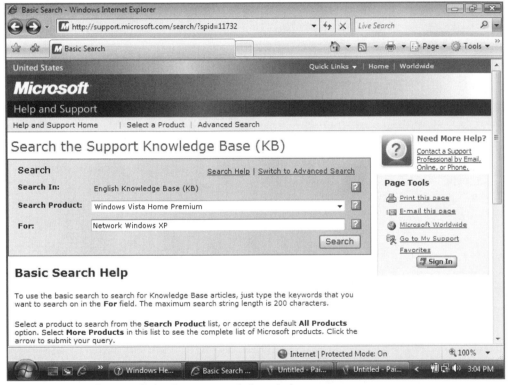

Figure A-6 Use the Knowledge Base to search for solutions on your own.

You an also perform advanced searches. With an advanced search you get to specifically state the following:

- Product name
- Key words
- What products to show results for

- Where to search (by full text, title only, and article ID or by error message)
- How to search (by using all the words entered, any of the words entered, or an exact phrase or by using And and Or options)
- The date the article was last modified
- How many results to show per page

You can also select what kinds of results you'd like to see (you must select one or more):

- How-to articles
- Downloads
- Troubleshooting
- Guided help
- Microsoft Office Online content
- Internet Explorer online Help content
- Windows Vista online Help content
- MSDN content
- TechNet content

For more help on using advanced searches, visit *http://support.microsoft.com/search/ ?adv=1.*

Join the Windows Vista Community

For general help using Windows Vista, visit the Windows Vista home page. It's at *www.microsoft.com/windows/products/windowsvista/default.mspx.* You can also visit the Windows Vista Community Web site at *http://windowshelp.microsoft.com/Windows/ en-US/community/* (for U.S. users), which offers a place to join user groups, read articles, and ask questions in one of the many Windows communities. You can also access blogs, meet the Windows Vista experts, view events, and even find and join a user group in your local area.

For information on networking, locate the Columns link, and search for columns on networking. An article you might be particularly interested in is the one on ad hoc networking. Not only can you find out why you'd need an ad hoc network but also how to set one up! The Windows Vista Community Web site offers a wealth of information.

Post and Search in Windows Communities

Go to the Windows Vista Community Web site, and locate the link to the Windows Vista Community discussion groups.

A discussion group (also called a *newsgroup*) is a place on the Internet where people communicate with each other by posting and reading messages about topics that interest them. The discussion groups at Microsoft are generally technical and trouble-shooting in nature.

A discussion group contains *discussion threads*, which are related messages. When a person posts a message, it is either to respond to an earlier post (in a thread) or to create a new one, thus creating a new thread. Anyone can access messages posted to newsgroups.

The discussion group you'll be interested in is likely the Windows Vista Networking and Sharing group. Here are some tips for working with discussion communities:

- Log in. You'll get to respond to messages that way. If you don't log in, you can only read the messages.

- Search for posts that may answer your question prior to posting your own message.

- To expand a thread, click the + sign. This allows you to view all the messages in the thread.

- To read a post by a particular author, click the name of an author in the thread pane.

- To collapse a thread and view only the thread summary, click the – sign at the top of the thread.

- To view an entire thread in its own window, double-click any post in a thread or the subject of the original post in the thread.

- If you write a post in ALL UPPERCASE LETTERS, people will think you're shouting.

- Create a meaningful subject line that describes in a few words what your post is about.

- Make your post as short as possible, but include details such as operating system, edition, computer make and model, and so on.

- Don't post the same message to more than one discussion group at the same time. This is called *cross-posting*.

- Be polite, no matter who may be impolite to you.

Contact Microsoft Customer Support

There is an option to contact Microsoft Customer Support. To view the Microsoft support options, go to *http://support.microsoft.com*, and from the Quick Links drop-down list, under Contact Support, click Select A Product. Click Windows Vista, and from the list, select your Windows Vista edition. This should be a last resort, though. You can get support in lot of other ways without having to pay for it!

Once you've selected the product you need help with, you're offered support choices. Although this may change in the future, for now there are three choices: E-Mail Support, Individual Chat Support, and Phone Support.

E-MAIL SUPPORT

Response time for e-mail support is one business day. The 90-day no-charge support begins as follows:

- From the date you place your first support request

- For Windows Vista, from the date you activate the product

Once the no-charge period ends, most incidents cost $59, although some support may not be covered under this charge. You'll have to agree to the terms of service and then select a computer that you want assistance with. You may be prompted to install ActiveX controls. If prompted, perform the installation. You'll need your product identification number too. You can find that in the Welcome Center under View Computer Details. If you don't want to bother, you can let Microsoft pull the product number from your computer.

If the computer is still covered by the 90-grace period, you'll be prompted to type information related to your problem, along with other information. Provide all the information required. You can expect a response in one business day.

INDIVIDUAL CHAT SUPPORT

Response time for individual chat support is less than one minute. The 90-day no-charge support begins as follows:

- From the date you place your first support request
- For Windows Vista, from the date you activate the product

Once the no-charge period ends, most incidents cost $59, although some support may not be covered under this charge. You'll have to agree to the terms of service and then select a computer that you want assistance with. You may be prompted to install ActiveX controls. If prompted, perform the installation. You'll need your product identification number too. You can find that in the Welcome Center under View Computer Details. If you don't want to bother or can't find the number, you can let Microsoft pull the product number from your computer.

If the computer is still covered by the 90-grace period, you'll be prompted to type information related to your problem, along with other information. Provide all the information required.

PHONE SUPPORT

Response time for phone support varies depending on how busy the support center is and how many calls are ahead of you. The 90-day no-charge support begins as follows:

- From the date you place your first support request
- For Windows Vista, from the date you activate the product

Once the no-charge period is over, most incidents cost $59, although some support may not be covered under this charge. To get started, call 1-800-936-5700. TTY/TDD call 1-800-892-5234. Costs will vary.

Glossary

802.11a Specifies a wireless protocol that operates in the 5-gigahertz (GHz) range in the United States, which has been recently expanded to other frequencies. The 802.11a standard offers an enhanced data speed up to 54 megabits per second (Mbps) and became available after 802.11b.

802.11b A wireless protocol that boosts data speeds to 11 megabits per second (Mbps) in the frequency range of about 2.4 gigahertz (GHz).

802.11g A wireless protocol that operates in the 2.4-gigahertz (GHz) band, is compatible with 802.11b devices, and operates at up to 54 megabits per second (Mbps).

802.11n A higher-speed wireless network standard that is still under development. Several technologies called *pre-n* technologies claim to offer top speeds of 108, 240, and 350+ megahertz (MHz).

10Base-T A technology that allows networks to be created using twisted-pair cable, better known as *Ethernet cable*.

A

access point (AP) A network hardware device used to access network resources from a remote location such as a computer, and vice versa. Common access devices are routers and wireless access points.

ad hoc network A temporary network in which wireless devices directly communicate with each other. This type of network allows wireless devices within range of each other to locate and communicate without involving central access points.

adapter A hardware device that requests information from network devices and returns the results to the client. Common network adapters include network interface cards (NICs), wireless adapters, and wireless cards.

ADSL Stands for *asymmetric digital subscriber line*, which is an asymmetric high speed digital network connection that generally connects a home and an Internet service provider (ISP). This is a high-speed digital standard for voice, data, image, and video, and it transfers data across public networks using cell-relay technology. See also digital subscriber line (DSL) and symmetric digital subscriber line (SDSL).

antivirus software An application designed to protect from, identify, and remove known or potential computer viruses.

AppleTalk A set of communications protocols that defines networking on an AppleShare network.

authentication The process a computer or network server takes to determine the identity of a user that is attempting to access the computer or network.

B

bandwidth A measurement of how much data can be sent through a connection, usually measured in bits per second (bps).

baud A measurement of how many bits a modem can send or receive per second. This is an older term usually associated with telephone modems used with dial-up connections to the Internet.

bit A single-digit number in base-2, which is a 1 or a 0. A bit is the smallest unit of computerized data. Bandwidth is generally calculated in bits per second.

bits per second (bps) How fast data moves from one device to another. For instance, a 56-kilobyte (K) modem can move approximately 57,000 bits per second.

Bluetooth A technology that uses radio communications to wirelessly link devices over short distances. Uses include cell phones, personal digital assistants (PDAs), and wireless headsets. Bluetooth is not suggested for home network connections, because it was created and best applied to support simple wireless connections between personal consumer devices and peripherals. Bluetooth can cover only short distances, about 30 feet (10 meters). Bluetooth devices communicate at less than 1 megabits per second (Mbps).

bridge A device that connects two or more physical networks and forwards data between them. Bridges can usually be made to filter data, which means you can decide what data is transferred between the networks and what is not.

broadband In home networking, refers to connections to the Internet that are much faster than any speed you can get with a modem. Speeds of a broadband connections vary. Broadband has become synonymous with any Internet connection that involves a digital subscriber line (DSL) or cable modem (and sometimes a satellite connection).

broadband modem A digital modem used with broadband service. Cable and digital subscriber line (DSL) modems are almost always supplied by the Internet service provider and are included in the provider's monthly service fee.

broadband router A router that combines the features of a network switch, a firewall, and a Dynamic Host Configuration Protocol (DHCP) server. Broadband routers make setting up a home network simple by automatically supporting file sharing, media sharing, Internet connection sharing, and network gaming. Traditional broadband routers incorporate Ethernet cables, which connect the router, the broadband modem, and each computer on a wired home network.

C

carrier A third-party provider of communications services by wire, fiber, or radio. See Internet service provider (ISP).

Category 5 (Cat 5) The fifth Ethernet cable standard for twisted-pair Ethernet cabling and currently the most popular.

Category 6 (Cat 6) The sixth Ethernet cable standard for twisted-pair Ethernet cabling and gaining in popularity.

coaxial cable (coax) A cable used for high-frequency transmission of telephone, telegraph, and television signals. In home networking, coaxial cable is what connects the cable modem to the cable outlet in the wall.

crossover cable A cable used to directly connect two devices of the same type to each other over Ethernet. This creates a wired ad hoc network. Ethernet crossover cables are generally used when you need to temporarily network two computers without involving a network router, switch, or hub.

D

digital subscriber line (DSL) A popular transmission method for moving data over regular phone lines. You can subscribe to DSL from any DSL Internet server provider for a monthly fee. DSL requires that a DSL modem be connected and installed.

direct connection A permanent connection between a computer system and a network.

distributed network A network where processing tasks are shared among different parts of the network. Processing may be shared by local computers, file servers, print servers, application servers, and database servers. This

enhances performance because hardware can be assigned specific roles depending on the type of work to be done. A NetWare network is an example of a distributed network.

domain On the Internet, a domain is a set of network addresses organized in levels including the top level, second level, third level, and so on. The top level at *www.microsoft.com* is the Microsoft home page. Secondary levels include *www.microsoft.com/windowsvista*. Lower levels exist as well.

In networking terms, a domain is a set of network resources, including servers, applications, computers, printers, and so on. Users log on to the domain to access these resources. Domains are much more secure than workgroups and require at least one domain controller to create.

domain controller A computer configured and used to manage the master user database for the domain, which includes such things as user names, permissions, and other user data. Domains have at least one primary domain controller and often one or more backup domain controllers. Setting up and maintaining domain controllers is a time-consuming activity and generally requires a full-time administrator when implemented in larger companies.

domain name The unique name that identifies a Web site, computer, or resource on the Internet. Microsoft.com is a domain name. Domain names always have two or more parts, and each part is separated by a single dot.

Domain Name System (DNS) The system that translates Internet domain names into Internet Protocol (IP) numbers. DNS is what allows you to type a friendly name such as *www.microsoft.com*, instead of typing the actual 32-bit IP address of the Web site. A DNS server is a server that performs the conversion.

dotted decimal notation The system for how Internet Protocol (IP) addresses are written. Dotted decimal notation consists of four sets of numbers separated by periods, as in 200.155.61.12. Although you can access a Web site or network resources using this number, it's easier to remember and access the resource using its friendly name, such as *www.microsoft.com*.

Dynamic DNS (DDNS) DDNS is a service that associates Internet domain names to Internet Protocol (IP) addresses. Unlike the Domain Name System (DNS), DDNS works with dynamic IP addressing. This is a great technology for home network users, who usually receive dynamic, frequently changing Internet Protocol (IP) addresses from their ISPs.

Dynamic Host Configuration Protocol (DHCP) A protocol by which a computer obtains an Internet Protocol (IP) number (and other network information) from a server on the local network and thus becomes part of that network. A DHCP server can be configured to automatically assign addresses, known as *automatic IP addressing*, or provide an unchanging address, called *static IP addressing*.

dynamic IP address A temporary IP address given to a computer or network resource for the duration of the network session.

E

Ethernet A technology that allows users to physically connect computers on a home network using Ethernet cable. Ethernet is the most widely used local area network (LAN) standard. Most Ethernet transmits data at 10 or 100 megabits per second (Mbps). (See Fast Ethernet.)

extranet A private network that uses Internet technology to make available part of its network so outsiders such as suppliers and venders have access.

F

Fast Ethernet An Ethernet technology that supports a maximum data rate of 100 megabits per second (Mbps).

fiber optics A data transmission method that sends data over fiber-optic cables. Data is transmitted at the speed of light and thus produces an extremely quick method to transfer data. Fiber-optic technology can and does bring ultra-high-speed Internet service—100 megabits per second (Mbps) and faster—to residential neighborhoods; however, the service can be quite expensive.

fiber-optic cable A networking cable that consists of strands of glass fibers inside an insulated casing. These cables carry data over very long distances and at a very high rate of speed, and they send data at the speed of light.

file sharing A networking feature that allows more than one person to access the same file at the same time.

File Transfer Protocol (FTP) The Internet protocol used to transfer files between host computers. FTP is a common method of moving files between two Internet sites because FTP offers an easy way to log in to another Internet site to transfer or retrieve files and is a widely accepted protocol.

firewall A hardware or software solution that separates a network into two or more parts for the purpose of scanning the data that goes in and out and rejecting data that is deemed harmful. A firewall and router combination looks at each network packet to determine whether to forward it across the firewall to the other network resources.

FireWire A high-performance networking standard from Apple that is similar to USB. Most people use FireWire cables to connect hardware such as digital video cameras. You can, however, connect two computers with a FireWire cable and share data between them. FireWire operates at speeds of 400 megabits per second (Mbps).

G

gateway A hardware or software configuration that translates between two different protocols, such as a router that sends and receives data between your home network and the Internet. A gateway is often referred to as a network *exit* point.

gateway address The IP address of the gateway.

Gigabit Ethernet An extension of the Ethernet communication standard. The Gigabit Ethernet standard supports a theoretical maximum data rate of 1,000 megabits per second (Mbps).

gigabits per second (Gbps) A unit of data transfer rate equal to 1,000 megabits per second, 1 million kilobits per second, or 1 billion bits per second.

gigabyte 1,000 or 1,024 megabytes, depending on who you ask.

gigahertz (GHz) The transmission frequency of radio signals in cycles per second; 1 gigahertz equals one billion cycles per second, or 1,000 MHz.

Gopher A network similar to the World Wide Web but less versatile and generally used only for text files.

guest A network computer that accesses services from another computer on the network. When connecting to a computer using Remote Desktop, the computer you connect to is called the *host*, and the connecting computer is called the *guest*.

H

hacker A term used denote a person who tries and often succeeds in breaking into a computer system or network.

hop One portion of the path a data packet must take to get from the source computer to the destination computer. When data is transmitted over the Internet, the data hops from router to router to get to its destination.

host A network computer that offers services to other computers on the network. When connecting to a computer using Remote Desktop, the computer you connect to is called the *host*, and the connecting computer is called the *guest*.

hosting A term used to define a Web site or service that maintains resources on behalf of clients. Hosting is generally provided by large companies that store, maintain, and publish Web pages created by end users.

hotspot A location where a wireless network is publicly available. Most of the time, a connection to the Internet is provided too. You'll find hotspots in airports, hotels, and coffee shops, among others. Hotspots are public networks, so users should take precautions when connecting.

hub A small, simple, inexpensive network device that joins multiple computers together. Hubs contain "stations" where Ethernet cables can be attached. Hubs come in four-station, six-station, and eight-station models, among others.

Hypertext Transfer Protocol (HTTP) The protocol for moving Hypertext Markup Language (HTML) files across the Internet. HTTP is the most necessary protocol used on the Web. File Transfer Protocol (FTP) is another type of protocol.

I

infrared Electromagnetic waves whose frequency range is below that of the visible spectrum and above that of microwaves.

Infrared Data Association (IrDA) An association that establishes standards for the exchange of data over infrared waves. The IrDA standard has been widely adopted by PC and consumer electronics manufacturers.

Integrated Services Digital Network (ISDN) A technology that combines voice and digital network services. With ISDN, customers can access digital data services as well as voice connections through a single wire.

Internet A collection of networks interconnected by routers and incorporating TCP/IP addressing. Tens of thousands of computers are connected to the Internet.

Internet address A 32-bit address given to and associated with Internet hosts using TCP/IP. Although you can connect to an Internet host using its 32-bit address (such as 100.251.4.25), you use its friendly name instead. (See dotted decimal notation.)

Internet Connection Sharing (ICS) A technology that lets a computer connect directly to the Internet, often through dial-up, and then share its Internet connection with others on a network.

Internet Control Message Protocol (ICMP) The protocol used to handle errors and control messages across Transmission Control Protocol/Internet Protocol (TCP/IP) networks such as the Internet.

Internet Protocol (IP) A network layer protocol for the Internet protocol suite. Every client, server, and device on a network must have a unique IP address to distinguish it from other hosts on the network.

Internet Protocol (IP) number A unique number consisting of four parts separated by dots. Every machine on the Internet must have a unique IP number to participate and be part of the network.

intranet A private network that is contained in a larger network. The main purpose of an intranet is to share company information and resources among employees. Often an intranet will use a virtual private network (VPN) to incorporate added security for connections made by employees.

K

kilobit 1,024 or 1,000 bits, depending on who you ask.

kilobits per second (Kbps) Data transfer rates are measured in kilobits per second; a kilobit is 1,000 bits.

kilobyte 1,000 bytes or 1,024 bytes, depending on who you ask.

L

leased line A network connection that is rented for the exclusive use from your location to another location. The highest-speed data connections require a leased line, which include T-1 and T-3.

local area network (LAN) A computer network limited to a small area, usually in the same building or a floor of a building. Home networks are LANs.

login Often an account name used to gain access to a computer system. *Logging in* also refers to the process of connecting to a computer or a network by inputting your specific user name and password.

M

malware Any program or file that can harm a computer, which includes but is not limited to viruses, worms, Trojan horses, and spyware. Malware is short for *malicious software*.

Media Access Control (MAC) address In any network, the MAC address is any computer's unique hardware number. Every computer has a unique number. When you connect to the Internet, a system exists that associates your Internet Protocol (IP) address to your computer's physical (MAC) address on the LAN.

megabit One million bits.

megabits per second (Mbps) A measure of bandwidth that represents how many millions of bits per second data is transferred.

megabyte 1,000 kilobytes, or 1,024 kilobytes, depending on who you ask. Also, one million bytes.

megahertz (MHz) One million hertz.

metropolitan area network (MAN) A network that connects computers and other resources over a large area, such as a city or school district.

modem A hardware device that connects a computer to the Internet through a phone line. The bandwidth for modem over regular telephone lines is about 57,000 bit per second (bps). The term comes from MOdulator/DEModulator.

N

network A collection of computers, printers, servers, and other devices connected in a way that allows them to share information and resources.

network address A unique identifier for a computer on a network. One of the best known types of network addressing Internet Protocol (IP) addressing. An IP addresses consist of 32 bits of data in dotted decimal notation that uniquely identifies all computers on the network.

Network Address Translation (NAT) A technology that allows a local area network

to use one set of Internet Protocol (IP) addresses for internal traffic and a second set of addresses for external traffic. NAT is provided with Windows Internet Connection Sharing. NAT enables network administrators to enact a firewall by hiding internal IP addresses from the Internet and other networks and also reduces the need for purchasing additional external IP addresses.

Network Basic Input Output System (NetBIOS) A program that allows computers to communicate within a local area network. It is the standard interface for networks on IBM PC and compatible systems.

network interface card (NIC) A hardware card installed into a computer's motherboard so the computer can connect to a network. Most computers come with NICs built in. Personal computers usually include a network interface card specifically designed for the local area network (LAN) transmission technology used, such as Ethernet.

node Any single computer connected to a network.

noise Static (interference) between two points in a transmission circuit.

P

packet A unit of data sent from one computer to another. Packets are created when large amounts of data are broken up into smaller ones to make sending the data possible. Each packet is numbered and includes the destination address. Data packets may travel different routes through the Internet to get to their destination address; however, once they arrive, they are reassembled into the original file.

password A group of letters, numbers, and characters used to used to log in to a computer or network.

passphrase A collection of letters, numbers, and characters used to control access to a network or computer. In the context of this book, a passphrase is used in setting up wireless home networks and helps secure the network from unwanted visitors.

peer-to-peer (P2P) A network in which all computers are treated as equals. Individuals can share their computers' hard drives, CD-ROM drives, and other storage devices with other computers on the network. P2P networks are often used to share software, music, and other files with others on the Internet. One of the most famous P2P networks was the original form of Napster.

peer-to-peer communication The communications that occur when two computers are directly connected without any intermediary devices.

physical topology The physical layout of the network, including how the cables are arranged and computers are connected.

port A place where information goes into or out of a computer, such as a USB port or an Apple FireWire port. A port can also be a

modem or where an Ethernet cable is physically connected to a PC. Basically, a port is a connection point for a cable.

protocol A formal set of rules that must be followed for computers and networks to exchange information.

proxy server A computer that sits in between a user's computer and a computer or network the user wants to access. When a proxy server is established, the user's computer makes all of its requests for data from the proxy server, and the proxy server then makes requests from the computer that contains it. This adds an extra layer of security to the network and is often incorporated in local area networks (LANs).

R

repeater A device used in a network to strengthen a signal as it passes through the network cable.

RJ-45 The connectors used for the ends of unshielded twisted-pair cable.

router A computer, software application, or piece of hardware that handles data being sent between two networks. Routers look at the source and destination addresses of the data packets passing through and decide which route to use to send them. In home networking, a router is usually a hardware device that routes data from the local area network (LAN) to the Internet.

S

satellite Internet service A subscription service most often used to access the Internet when a broadband connection is unavailable.

security certificate Security information often stored as a text file that is used to establish a secure connection employing the Secure Sockets Layer (SSL) protocol.

segment A section of cable on a network. In Ethernet networks, you can have a trunk segment (which has one or more computers attached to it) or a link segment (which connects a computer to another device, such as a repeater).

server Most often a computer that provides a specific kind of service to client computers. For instance, there are mail servers, print servers, Internet servers, and data servers, all of which provide a service to users on a network. Servers are most often used in domains, but workgroups can have servers as well (such as Windows Home Server).

service set identifier (SSID) The name of your wireless network.

smart card A small plastic card with a microchip that is loaded with data and used for establishing a user's identity when logging on to a computer or network.

spyware Software that is installed on a user's computer without the user's knowledge. Spyware often monitors the use of the computer without the user's knowledge or consent and can acquire personal information or copy keystrokes. Spyware is usually obtained while installing other software; music sharing software is a popular medium.

stand-alone A computer that is not connected to a network.

static Internet Protocol address An Internet Protocol (IP) address that never changes.

switch A more sophisticated device than a network hub, a network switch can determine the destination MAC address and store this address for future use. As more data is acquired, it can forward the incoming data directly to the destination. This alone makes a switch more effective than a hub.

symmetric digital subscriber line (SDSL) A version of DSL where the upload and download speeds are equal.

T

T-1 A leased-line connection that can transmit data at 1,544,000 bits per second. T-1 lines are commonly used to connect large networks to the Internet and are generally too expensive for home users.

T-3 A leased-line connection that can transmit data at 44,736,000 bits per second. Although less expensive than T-1, it is still much more expensive than other options such as fiber-optic or broadband.

Telnet A virtual terminal protocol for the Internet. This allows users to log in to a remote computer and work at that computer as if they were actually sitting in front of it.

terabyte 1,000 gigabytes.

terminal A device, usually a keyboard and a display screen, that allows you to send commands to a computer located somewhere else. Airports are starting to incorporate terminals in which passengers can print their own boarding passes and itineraries by accessing the data on a main computer, without actually sitting in front of it.

Terminal Server client A computer that connects to a host using a remote connection. In Remote Desktop, the Terminal Server client is the one connecting to the remote PC.

throughput A measurement of how fast data can travel through a specific transmission medium.

Transmission Control Protocol/Internet Protocol (TCP/IP) The set of protocols that transfers data on the Internet. TCP/IP software is included with every major kind of computer operating system and is required to obtain direct access to the Internet.

Trojan horse A program that pretends to do, or does, something useful, but in reality contains malicious code that can harm the computer. A Trojan horse is the network equivalent of a computer virus.

tunnel The path established by one network to send its data via another network's connections using a VPN connection.

twisted Pair A form of wiring in which two conductors are wound together to cancel out electromagnetic interference (EMI) and crosstalk from neighboring wires.

U

uniform resource locator (URL) The address to a file on the Internet. URLs can be typed into a Web browser or embedded within Web pages as hypertext links. An example of a URL is *www.microsoft.com*.

V

very high bitrate digital subscriber line (VDSL) A data transmission speed that ranges from 25 to 50 megabits per second (Mbps) and is used only over very short distances.

virtual private network (VPN) A network that uses the Internet to transmit encrypted data, making the network seem as though it's private and thus much more difficult to hack into.

virus Replicating and harmful computer code. A virus will copy itself and may display messages, delete files, rename files, change Web browser home pages, and more. Viruses spread by attaching themselves to programs and files and are often transferred within files sent through email.

Voice over Internet Protocol (VoIP) A technology used to make telephone calls over the Internet.

W

wide area network (WAN) A network that covers a large area, such as a network that extends beyond a single building or college campus. The Internet is a WAN, as are company networks that span cities, states, and even countries.

Wired Equivalent Privacy (WEP) A security system that uses keys on both sides of the transmission to encrypt data and offer secure transmission This provides a minimal level of security and privacy. WEP is weak, and other security options provide better safety.

Wireless Application Protocol (WAP) A set of protocols that standardizes the way wireless devices can be used for Internet access, including accessing e-mail, the Internet, newsgroups, and more.

Wireless fidelity (Wi-Fi) A popular term for wireless data communication.

workgroup A collection of computers, printers, and perhaps servers, connected in a local area network, that communicate and exchange data and resources with one another.

workstation A computer connected to a network.

worm A virus that does not infect other programs but instead makes copies of itself and infects other network computers. A worm might also harm files and programs.

World Wide Web (WWW) A term used to describe the Internet.

Index

Symbols and Numbers

$ (dollar) symbol, 110, 115
10Base-T, 239
802.11a standard
    choosing, 64–65
    configuring Xbox 360, 174–175
    defined, 12, 239
802.11b standard
    choosing, 64–65
    configuring wireless settings, 67
    defined, 12, 239
802.11g standard
    choosing, 64–65
    configuring wireless settings, 67
    defined, 12, 239
802.11n standard, 12, 64, 239

A

access points (APs)
    connecting to Internet using, 19
    defined, 239
    optimal placement of, 221–222
    overview of, 12–13
    routers compatible with, 12
ad hoc networks, 239
adapters, network
    defined, 239
    NICs as. *see* network interface cards (NICs)
    wireless. *see* wireless adapters
    wireless cards as, 8, 70, 72

add-ins, Windows Home Server, 157
administrator accounts
    creating, 95
    overview of, 93–94
    protecting files when there are multiple, 113
ADSL (asymmetric digital subscriber), 239
advanced account properties, 99–100
Advanced Sharing, folders, 113–115
Advanced tab, printer Properties dialog, 131–132
Advanced tab, Remote Desktop, 195–196
Advanced tab, Windows Firewall, 25, 215
Airport, 74–75
alerts, security, 202
Allow permission
    advanced permission levels using, 116
    folder sharing, 114–115
    printer sharing, 128–129
Allowed Items, Windows Defender, 29
antivirus software, 203, 239
AppleTalk, 239
asymmetric digital subscriber (ADSL), 239
authentication, 195–196, 239

B

backups
    configuring Windows Home Server, 143,
        154–156
    performing monthly, 221
    using Windows Backup and Restore Center,
        215–220

bandwidth
    calculating in bits per second, 240
    calculating in megabits per second, 246
    defined, 240
    for modems over telephone lines, 246
baud, 240
bit, 240
bits per second (bps), 240
Bluetooth technology, 40, 240
boot order, hardware, 50, 69
bridges, 240
broadband
    configuring Windows Vista–based PC for, 19
    defined, 13, 240
broadband modems
    defined, 240
    setting up for Ethernet networks, 46
    setting up for wireless networks, 66
broadband routers
    connecting server to, 159
    defined, 11, 240
    purchasing equipment and, 14
    Windows Home Server requirement, 142
broadband transmission, 13

C

cable
    biannual check of, 221
    Cat 5, 13, 240
    Cat 6, 240
    coaxial, 240
    direct connection, 6–7, 35–36
    Easy Transfer, 7
    Ethernet. *see* Ethernet cable
    Ethernet crossover, 6–7, 41, 240
    null modem, 6, 40
    parallel interlink, 40
    USB-to-USB direct link, 7, 41

cable modems
    boot order and, 69
    connecting, 46
    connecting for wireless networks, 66, 68
    connecting hub to, 47–48
carriers, 240
Category 5 (Cat 5) cable, 13, 240
Category 6 (Cat 6) cable, 240
certificates, file encryption, 99
Channel setting, wireless network, 67
coaxial cable (coax), 240
conflicts, sync, 170
connections
    Remote Desktop, 187–191
    troubleshooting Windows Home Server,
        146–149
    verifying working, 221
    Windows Home Server, 142
Contributor permission, 109
Co-Owner permission, 109
costs, new equipment, 14
crossover cable
    adding Windows XP–based PC to network, 41
    cost of using for direct connections, 9
    defined, 240
    overview of, 6–7

D

data backups, 215–218
DDNS (Dynamic DNS), 242
Deny permission
    advanced permission levels using, 116
    folder sharing, 114
    printer sharing, 128–129
Device Manager, 148–149
devices, viewing, 86–88
DHCP (Dynamic Host Configuration Protocol)
    servers, 240

dial-up connection, 19, 241
digital subscriber line (DSL)
    adding Windows XP–based PC to wired network
        using, 57
    ADSL, 239
    broadband and, 13, 240
    connecting Ethernet hardware, 46–48
    connecting for wireless networks, 66, 68
    defined, 241
    router connecting to, 12
    SDSL, 248
    VDSL, 249
direct connection, 33–43
    adding second Windows Vista–based PC, 39
    adding Windows XP–based PC, 39–42
    connecting older PCs, 43
    creating password-protected account,
        42–43
    creating workgroup names, 34
    defined, 241
    hardware for, 9
    overview of, 6–7, 33
    physically connecting two PCs, 35–36
    sharing host's network connection, 38–39
    Turn On Network Discovery on Windows
        Vista–based PC, 36–38
direct link cables, 7
Display tab, Remote Desktop, 192–193
distributed network, 241
DNS (Domain Name System), 13, 242
dollar ($) symbol, 110, 115
domain controller, 241
domain name, 241
Domain Name System (DNS), 13, 242
domains, 52, 241
dotted decimal notation, 242
drivers, printer, 124–127

drives
    data backups to network, 218–219
    defragmenting hard, 222
    Windows Home Server installation,
        144–145
Dynamic DNS (DDNS), 242
Dynamic Host Configuration Protocol
    (DHCP) servers
    adding Mac to wireless network, 74–75
    broadband routers using features of, 240
    configuring Mac for wired network, 59
    defined, 240
dynamic IP addresses, 242

E

Easy Transfer cables, 7
EFS (Encrypting File System), 113, 120
e-mail, changing permissions, 112
Encrypting File System (EFS), 113, 120
encryption
    file encryption certificates, 99
    wireless network settings, 68
errors, sync, 169
Ethernet, 45–62
    adding PCs, 55–61
    connecting hardware, 46–50
    creating private network, 52–53
    crossover cable. see crossover cable
    defined, 13, 242
    hardware for, 9–11
    naming, 50–52
    overview of, 7–8, 45–46
    setting up direct connection, 35–36
    troubleshooting Windows Home Server,
        148–149
    turning on network discovery, 53–54
    understanding boot order for hardware, 50
    Windows Home Server requirements, 142–143

Ethernet cable
adding Windows Vista–based PC to network, 55
adding wireless router, 68
checking biannually, 237
connecting hub or switch, 47–48
connecting server to broadband router, 159
connecting Xbox 360 to network, 175
handling PCs without port for, 49
overview of, 9–10
Everyone group, printer sharing, 129
Experience tab, Remote Desktop, 194–195
extranet, 242

F

Fast Ethernet
defined, 242
speed of 802.11n comparable to, 64
transmission speed of, 45
Fast User Switching, 98
fiber optics, 242
fiber-optic cable, 243
File Encryption Wizard, 99
file sharing
choosing Public or Personal folders, 110
configuring Mac for, 58–59
defined, 243
setting up network for, 36, 80
working with shared folders, 106–108
File Transfer Protocol (FTP), 243
firewalls
broadband routers consisting of, 240
defined, 13, 243
Windows Home Server requirement, 142
Windows Security Center and, 200
FireWire, 243
folders. see shared folders
Full Control permission, 114, 117

G

Games settings, Parental Controls, 103
gateway
defined, 243
private networks including, 52
residential, 57
Terminal Services, 212
gateway address, 243
General tab, Offline Files settings, 163, 166
General tab, Remote Desktop settings, 192
General tab, Windows Firewall settings, 24, 213–214
General tab, Windows Home Server settings, 156
Gigabit Ethernet, 243
gigabits per second (Gbps), 243
gigabyte, 243
gigahertz (GHz), 243
Gopher, 243
guest
defined, 94, 243
remote access, 187
Remote Assistance vs. Remote Desktop, 185
turning on network discovery, 36–38
user account, 94–95

H

hackers, 244
hardware
boot order for, 50
direct connection, 9
Ethernet, 9–11, 46–50
before purchasing new, 13–14
speed of data dependent upon, 45
taking care of, 220–222
Windows Home Server requirements, 141–142
wireless, 11–13, 65–70
healthy networks, maintaining, 198–222
taking care of hardware, 220–222
User Account Control, 204–206

virus protection, 203–204
with Windows Backup and Restore Center,
215–220
with Windows Defender, 210–212
with Windows Firewall, 213–215
Windows Home Server, 158–159
with Windows Security Center, 198–202
with Windows Update, 206–209
History option, Windows Defender, 29
hop, 244
host
defined, 244
setting up Remote Desktop on, 183–186
sharing Internet connection of, 38–39
turning on network discovery, 36–38
hosting, 244
hotspot, 244
HTTP (HyperText Transfer Protocol), 244
hub
connecting Ethernet networks, 7, 47–49
defined, 244
overview of, 10
HyperText Transfer Protocol (HTTP), 244

I

ICMP (Internet Control Message Protocol), 245
icons
shared offline folder, 165
shared printer, 82
ICS (Internet Connection Sharing), 245
infrared
adding Windows XP–based PC using, 41–42
connecting two computers using, 7
defined, 244
Infrared Data Association (IrDA), 201
Integrated Services Digital Network (ISDN), 244

Internet
address, 244
configuring Windows Vista–based PC for, 19
defined, 244
sharing host's connection to, 38–39
using VPN to connect to, 183
Internet Connection Sharing (ICS), 245
Internet Control Message Protocol (ICMP), 245
Internet options, Windows Security Center Task
pane, 201
Internet Protocol (IP), 245
Internet Protocol (IP) number, 245
intranet, 201–202, 245
IP (Internet Protocol), 245
IP (Internet Protocol) number, 245
IP addresses, 13, 183
IrDA (Infrared Data Association), 244
ISDN (Integrated Services Digital Network), 244
Itanium-based computers, 125

K

kilobit, 245
kilobits per second (Kbps), 245
kilobyte, 245

L

leased lines, 245
List Folder Contents permission, NTFS, 117
local area network (LAN), 13, 245
Local Resources tab, Remote Desktop, 193
log off, user account, 92
login
defined, 245
to new standard account, 97–98
user account, 92

M

Mac
    adding to Ethernet network, 58–61
    adding to wireless network, 74–75
    using Remote Desktop, 182
MAC (Media Access Control) address, 245
maintenance. *see* healthy networks, maintaining
malware
    defined, 245
    Windows Defender removing, 211
    working with Windows Security Center, 200
Manage Documents permission, 127
Manage Printers permission, 128
MANs (metropolitan area networks), 246
Mbps (megabits per second), 246
media
    sharing, 84–85
    streaming with Windows Home Server Console,
        140–141
    syncing music, 167
Media Access Control (MAC) address, 245
media extenders
    defined, 173
    using Xbox as. *see* Xbox 360
media sharing
    types of media for, 178
    in Windows Home Server, 157
    in Windows Media Player 11, 177–178
    in Windows Vista–based PC for Xbox 360,
        176–177
megabit, 245
megabits per second (Mbps), 246
megabyte, 246
megahertz (MHz), 246
metropolitan area network (MAN), 246
Microsoft SpyNet, 29, 211–212
Microsoft Windows. *see* Windows

mismatched documents, 132
mobile devices, and sync partnerships, 171–172
Mode setting, wireless networks, 67
modems
    defined, 14, 246
    Ethernet networks, 46
    wireless networks, 66, 68
Modify permission, NTFS, 117
monitoring, Windows Home Server, 140
music, syncing, 167

N

naming conventions
    standard user accounts, 95
    workgroups, 34, 50–52
nested folders, accessing, 110
NetBIOS (Network Basic Input Output System), 246
network address, 246
Network Address Translation (NAT), 246
Network and Sharing Center, 77–88
    adding Windows Vista–based PC, 39
    configuring network discovery, 79
    configuring Windows Vista–based PC for Xbox
        360, 176–177
    connecting Ethernet hardware, 48
    overview of, 77–78
    password protection, 84
    setting up network locations, 78–79
    settings for shared folders, 106–107
    sharing files, 80
    sharing host's network connection, 38
    sharing media, 84–85
    sharing printers, 82–83
    sharing public folders, 81–82
    Turn On Network Discovery in, 36
    view computers and devices, 86–88
Network Basic Input Output System (NetBIOS), 246

Network Critical icon, Windows Home Server, 158–159

network discovery
    configuring, 79
    setting up direct connection, 36–38
    setting up Ethernet networks, 53–54
    verifying for wireless networks, 69–70

Network icon, Notification area, 70–72

Network icon, Windows Home Server, 158

network interface cards (NICs)
    defined, 246
    Ethernet crossover cables using, 6–7
    overview of, 9
    purchasing for Ethernet cables, 49

networks, 3–15
    defined, 246
    before purchasing new equipment, 14–15
    reasons for, 4–5
    remote access. *see* remote access
    Remote Desktop, 182
    terminology, 13–14
    types of configurations, 5–8
    types of hardware, 8–13
    viewing or changing locations, 78–79
    what Windows Vista offers, 4

New Connection Wizard, 147

noise, 246

NT file system (NTFS)
    applying, 117–118
    configuring Windows Vista Ultimate with, 217–218
    printer sharing and, 128
    understanding, 116–117

null modem cables, 6, 40

O

offline files, 161–172
    configuring Sync Center, 167–170
    creating sync partnerships, 171–172
    enabling, 162–163
    selecting, 163–165
    Sync Center and synchronization, 166–167
    sync conflicts, 170
    understanding, 162
    viewing available, 166
    working offline, 165

online resources
    hardware for wireless networks, 65
    networking older PCs, 43
    virus protection, 203
    VPNs, 183
    Windows Defender, 29
    Windows Live OneCare, 203

operating systems, for Windows Home Server, 143

P

P2P (peer-to-peer), 247

packets, 246–247

parallel interlink cables, 40

parallel ports, 6

Parental Controls, 100–104

partnerships, sync, 171–172

passphrase, 67–68, 70–71, 247

password protected sharing, 84

passwords
    creating for new accounts, 42–43, 95–96
    creating reset disk for, 96–97
    defined, 247
    parental control, 100–102
    standard account, 98
    user account, 93, 97
    Windows Home Server, 145, 157
    Windows Security Center, 198–202

peer-to-peer (P2P), 247

peer-to-peer communication, 247

performance, 142

permissions
    applying to printer sharing, 127–130
    applying to shared folders, 108, 114–115
    default, 109–112
    security, 116–118
personal data, backing up, 217
personal folder sharing, 110–111
personalizing
    user accounts, 92
    workgroup names, 50–52
physical topology, 247
ports
    defined, 14, 247
    for Ethernet, 49
    for hubs, switches, and routers, 10–11
    for null modem cables, 6
    purchasing more than needed, 10–11
power using sharing, 113–115
pre-n technologies, 239
Print permission, 127
printer sharing, 121–136
    accessing local printer, 133–134
    adding printer drivers, 124–127
    applying security permissions, 127–130
    configuring advanced printer settings, 130–132
    connected to another PC, 135–136
    connecting to Windows Vista–based PC, 18–19
    properties, 82–83
    using Remote Desktop, 134
    with Windows Vista OS, 122–123
    with Windows XP OS, 124
Private networks, 52–53, 78–79
processors, 124–126
profiles, advanced settings for user, 99–100
Programs, Parental Controls, 103
Programs tab, Remote Desktop, 194

properties
    configuring Internet, 201
    setting advanced account, 99–100
    shared printer, 82–83
protocols, 247
proxy servers, 247
Public folders
    creating subfolders/shortcuts within, 81–82
    locating on computer, 81
    personal folders vs., 110–111
    sharing, 81–82
Public networks, 52, 78–79

Q
Quarantined Items, Windows Defender, 29

R
Read & Execute permission, NTFS, 117
Read permission, folder sharing, 114
Read permission, NTFS, 117
Reader permission, 109
rebooting, 220
Region setting, wireless networks, 67
remote access
    configuring Windows Home Server, 157
    with Remote Desktop. see Remote Desktop
Remote Assistance, 185–186
Remote Desktop, 181–196
    configuring advanced settings, 195–196
    configuring display settings, 192–193
    configuring Experience tab, 194–195
    configuring general settings, 192
    configuring local resources, 193
    configuring programs, 194
    connecting to computer on local network,
        187–189

connecting to remote computer using VPN, 190–191

creating virtual private network, 183

overview of, 181–182

printing to network printer from anywhere using, 134

vs. Remote Assistance, 185–186

setting up host PC, 183–186

system and network requirements, 182

Windows Firewall and connection to, 187

repair installations, 220

repeaters, 247

reports, Parental Control, 103–104

residential gateways, 57

Restore, with Windows Backup and Restore Center, 219–220

RJ-45, 247

routers

boot order for, 50

broadband. *see* broadband routers

defined, 247

for wired Ethernet networks, 7–8, 10–11, 49

wireless. *see* wireless routers

S

satellite Internet service, 248

satellite modems

connecting hub to, 47–48

for Ethernet, 46

for wireless networks, 66, 68

Scan option, Windows Defender, 29

schedules, sync, 170

security

certificates, 248

permissions, 116–118, 127–130

working with Windows Security Center, 198–202

segments, 248

separator pages, 132

serial ports, 6

Server Authentication, Remote Desktop, 195

servers, defined, 248

service set identifiers (SSIDs), 67, 248

Share permissions, printers, 127–128

shared folders, 105–120

accessing from Windows Vista–based PC, 118–119

accessing from Windows XP–based PC, 119

applying default permissions, 109–115

applying NTFS permissions, 116–118

default, 106–108

Encrypting File System technologies, 120

Public, 81–82

Public vs. personal, 110–111

in Windows Home Server, 152–154

Sharing and Discovery, 80

smart cards, 99, 248

Software Explorer, Windows Defender, 29

Special Permissions, 117, 128

spooling, print, 132

spyware

defined, 248

Microsoft Spyware community, 211–212

when to suspect, 204

Windows Defender scans for, 211

SSIDs (service set identifiers), 67, 248

stand-alone, 248

standard user account

creating, 94–97

creating shared folders, 106–107

defined, 94

login, 97–98

parental controls and, 101

static Internet Protocol address, 248

subfolders
    creating within Public folder, 81–82
    moving private data out of shared folders, 115
    shared folders and, 110
Switch User, working with, 97–98
switches
    broadband routers consisting of, 240
    connecting Ethernet networks, 7, 47–49
    defined, 248
    overview of, 10
symmetric digital subscriber line (SDSL), 248
Sync Center, 166–170
system data, backups, 217
System Restore, 220

T

T-1 leased-line connection, 248
T-3 leased-line connection, 248
TCP/IP (Transmission Control Protocol/Internet
    Protocol), 14, 249
technology, wireless, 8, 12, 64–65
Telnet, 248
terabyte, 249
terminal, 249
Terminal Services client (Tsclient), 189, 249
Terminal Services gateway server, Remote
    Desktop, 196
terminology, network, 13–14
throughput, defined, 249
time limits, Parental Controls, 102
Tools and Settings, Windows Defender, 28–29
Transmission Control Protocol/Internet Protocol
    (TCP/IP), 14, 249
transparent bridging, 10
Trojan horse, 249
troubleshooting, Windows Home Server,
    146–149

Tsclient (Terminal Services client), 189, 249
tunnel, defined, 249
twisted pair, 249

U

UAC. *see* User Account Control (UAC)
uniform resource locator (URL), 249
updates
    defined, 19
    working with Windows Security Center, 200
    working with Windows Update, 206–209
USB ports, 7, 19
USB-to-Ethernet converters, 7, 49
USB-to-USB direct link cables, 7, 41
User Account Control (UAC)
    firewall exceptions prompted by, 214–215
    managing network passwords in, 97
    turning on, 23–24
    working with, 204–206
User Account Wizard, 152
user accounts, 91–104
    configuring advanced properties, 99–100
    creating, 94–97
    creating for Windows Home Server, 150
    creating shared folders, 106–108
    logging on to, 97–98
    for networked PCs, 93
    overview of, 91–92
    setting parental controls, 100–103
    setting up for Remote Desktop, 185–186
    for single PCs, 92
    types of, 93–94
    viewing parental control reports, 103–104

V

VDSL (very high bitrate digital subscriber line), 249
very high bitrate digital subscriber line (VDSL), 249

virtual private network (VPN)
connecting to remote computer using, 190–191
creating for Remote Desktop, 183
defined, 249
viruses
defined, 249
getting latest information on, 202, 221
protecting computer from, 203–204
when to suspect, 204
Windows Defender protection from, 210–212
working with Windows Security Center, 200
Voice over Internet Protocol (VoIP), 249
VoIP (Voice over Internet Protocol), 249
VPN. see virtual private network (VPN)

W

WAP (Wireless Application Protocol), 250
WAPs (wireless access points), 12–13, 65–70
warnings, sync, 170
Web restrictions, Parental Controls, 101–102
WEP (Wired Equivalency Privacy)
configuring wireless settings, 68
connecting Xbox 360 to wireless network, 175
defined, 250
wide area networks (WANs), 14, 249
Wi-Fi (wireless fidelity), 175, 250
Wi-Fi Protected Access (WPA), 68, 175
Windows 2000
adding to wireless networks, 74
networking older PCs, 43
setting up Ethernet networks, 58
Windows Backup and Restore Center
backing up data fundamentals, 215–218
backing up to network drive, 218–219
restoring with, 219
testing biannually, 222
trying rebooting, System Restore and repair
installation first, 220

Windows Defender
changing settings, 212
configuring, 28–29
opening, 26–27
verifying running of, 27
working with, 210–211
Windows Firewall
advanced options, 215
with Advanced Security, 25–26
configuring firewall exceptions, 214–215
configuring general settings, 213–214
options, 24
overview of, 213
Remote Desktop connections and, 187
turning on and configuring, 24–25
Windows Home Server, 140–159
activating, 147
adding and viewing shared folders, 152–154
adding user account, 150–152
additional features, 159
configuring backup settings, 154–156
configuring settings, 156–158
configuring Windows Home Server Connector
software, 149–150
Connector Wizard, 149–150
installation and setup, 144–146
overview of, 140
system requirements, 141–143
troubleshooting, 146–149
understanding, 140–141
viewing health of, 158–159
Windows Live OneCare, 30, 203
Windows ME
adding to wireless network, 74
networking older PCs, 43
setting up Ethernet networks, 58
Windows Media Center, and Xbox 360, 174–177
Windows Media Player, 167, 177–178

Windows Mobile Device Center, 171–172

Windows Security Center, 198–202

Windows Update
    installing optional updates, 22–23
    obtaining and installing manually, 208–209
    overview of, 19–20
    turning on and configuring, 20–21
    verifying or changing settings, 206–208

Windows Vista, 18–24
    accessing shared folders from, 118–119
    adding Mac to Ethernet network, 59–61
    configuring Windows Defender, 26–29
    configuring Windows Firewall, 24–26
    configuring Windows Live OneCare, 30
    configuring Windows Update, 19–23
    connecting printers, 18–19
    connecting to Internet, 19
    for Ethernet networks, 55–56
    network features, 3
    printer sharing with, 122–123, 135–136
    setting up direct connection. *see* direct
        connection
    turning on User Account Control, 23–24
    for wireless networks, 70–72
    for Xbox 360, 176–177

Windows Vista Ultimate, 217–218

Windows Vista Web Filter, 101

Windows XP
    accessing shared folders from, 119
    adding to wireless network, 72–74
    connecting to Windows Vista–based PC,
        39–42
    creating workgroup names for direct
        connection, 34
    overview of, 124
    setting up Ethernet networks, 56–58

Wired Equivalency Privacy (WEP)
    configuring wireless settings, 68
    connecting Xbox 360 to wireless network, 175
    defined, 250

wireless access points (WAPs), 12–13, 65–70

wireless adapters
    adding Windows Vista–based PC to wireless
        network, 70
    adding Windows XP–based PC to wireless
        network, 72
    connecting hardware for wireless
        networks, 65–70
    defined, 8
    overview of, 11–12
    router compatibility with, 12

Wireless Application Protocol (WAP), 250

wireless cards
    adding Windows Vista–based PC to wireless
        network, 70
    adding Windows XP–based PC to wireless
        network, 72
    laptops using, 8

Wireless fidelity (Wi-Fi), 175, 250

wireless Internet, 19

wireless networks, 63–75
    adding Macs, 74–75
    adding Windows Vista–based PCs, 70–72
    adding Windows XP–based PCs, 72–74
    advantages of, 63
    boot order for hardware, 69
    choosing, 15
    connecting hardware, 65–70
    connecting Xbox 360 to, 174, 175
    getting started with, 64–65
    hardware for, 11–13

overview of, 8, 63–64

turn on network discovery, 69–70

wireless routers

boot order for, 69

defined, 12

installing, 65, 66

setting up physical connections, 68

Wireless Zero Configuration utility, 73

workgroup names

creating on Windows Vista or XP, 34

personalizing, 50–52

troubleshooting Windows Home Server, 146–147

workgroups, defined, 250

workstations, defined, 250

World Wide Web (WWW), 250

worms, 250

WPA (Wi-Fi Protected Access), 68, 175

Write permission, NTFS, 117

X

x64 processors, 125

x86 processors, 124

Xbox 360

configuring, 175

configuring Windows Vista–based PC for, 176–177

connecting to network, 175

as media extender, 174

media sharing in Windows Media Player 11, 177–178

network requirements, 174

types of media for sharing, 178

About the Author

Joli Ballew is a Microsoft Windows MVP, a technical author, a technology trainer, and a Web site manager in the Dallas area. She has several certifications, including Microsoft MVP, MCSE, A+, and MCDST. In addition to writing, she occasionally teaches computer classes at the local junior college and works as a network administrator and Web designer for North Texas Graphics. She has written almost two dozen books, including *Degunking Windows* (awarded the IPPY award for best computer book of the year in 2005), *PC Magazine's Office 2007 Solutions*, and *Breakthrough Windows Vista with Microsoft Press*. Joli also writes for Microsoft's Windows XP Expert Zone and the Windows Vista Community Web site, writes and gives Microsoft Webcasts, and is an occasional Microsoft blogger. Joli has also written a textbook for Microsoft's MCDST certification. In her free time, she enjoys golfing, doing yard work, exercising at the local gym, and teaching her cat, Pico, tricks.

Windows Vista™ Resources for Administrators

Windows Vista Administrator's Pocket Consultant

William Stanek
ISBN 9780735622968

Portable and precise, this pocket-sized guide delivers immediate answers for the day-to-day administration of Windows Vista. Featuring easy-to-scan tables, step-by-step instructions, and handy lists, this book offers the straightforward information you need to solve problems and get the job done—whether you're at your desk or in the field!

Windows Vista Resource Kit

Mitch Tulloch, Tony Northrup, Jerry Honeycutt, Ed Wilson, Ralph Ramos, and the Windows Vista Team
ISBN 9780735622838

Get the definitive reference for deploying, configuring, and supporting Windows Vista—from the experts who know the technology best. This guide offers in-depth, comprehensive technical guidance on automating deployment; implementing security enhancements; administering group policy, files folders, and programs; and troubleshooting. Includes an essential toolkit of resources on DVD.

MCTS Self-Paced Training Kit (Exam 70-620): Configuring Windows Vista Client

Ian McLean and Orin Thomas
ISBN 9780735623903

Get in-depth preparation plus practice for Exam 70-620, the required exam for the new Microsoft Certified Technology Specialist (MCTS): Windows Vista Client certification. This 2-in-1 kit focuses on installing client software and configuring system settings, security features, network connectivity, media applications, and mobile devices. Ace your exam prep—and build real-world job skills—with lessons, practice tests, evaluation software, and more.

MCITP Self-Paced Training Kit (Exam 70-622): Installing, Maintaining, Supporting, and Troubleshooting Applications on the Windows Vista Client – Enterprise

Tony Northrup and J.C. Mackin
ISBN 9780735624085

Maximize your performance on Exam 70-622, the required exam for the new Microsoft® Certified IT Professional (MCITP): Enterprise Support Technician certification. Comprehensive and in-depth, this 2-in-1 kit covers managing security, configuring networking, and optimizing performance for Windows Vista clients in an enterprise environment. Ace your exam prep—and build real-world job skills—with lessons, practice tests, evaluation software, and more.

MCITP Self-Paced Training Kit (Exam 70-623): Installing, Maintaining, Supporting, and Troubleshooting Applications on the Windows Vista Client – Consumer

Anil Desai with Chris McCain of GrandMasters
ISBN 9780735624238

Get the 2-in-1 training kit for Exam 70-623, the required exam for the new Microsoft Certified IT Professional (MCITP): Consumer Support Technician certification. This comprehensive kit focuses on supporting Windows Vista clients for consumer PCs and devices, including configuring security settings, networking, troubleshooting, and removing malware. Ace your exam prep—and build real-world job skills—with lessons, practice tests, evaluation software, and more.

See more resources at **microsoft.com/mspress**
and **microsoft.com/learning**

2007 Microsoft® Office System Resources for Developers and Administrators

Microsoft Office SharePoint® Server 2007 Administrator's Companion

Bill English with the Microsoft SharePoint Community Experts
ISBN 9780735622821

Get your mission-critical collaboration and information management systems up and running. This comprehensive, single-volume reference details features and capabilities of SharePoint Server 2007. It delivers easy-to-follow procedures, practical workarounds, and key troubleshooting tactics—for on-the-job results.

Microsoft Windows SharePoint Services Version 3.0 Inside Out

Errin O'Connor
ISBN 9780735623231

Conquer Microsoft Windows SharePoint Services— from the inside out! This ultimate, in-depth reference packs hundreds of time-saving solutions, troubleshooting tips, and workarounds. You're beyond the basics, so now learn how the experts tackle information sharing and team collaboration— and challenge yourself to new levels of mastery!

Microsoft SharePoint Products and Technologies Administrator's Pocket Consultant

Ben Curry
ISBN 9780735623828

Portable and precise, this pocket-sized guide delivers immediate answers for the day-to-day administration of Sharepoint Products and Technologies. Featuring easy-to-scan tables, step-by-step instructions, and handy lists, this book offers the straightforward information you need to get the job done—whether you're at your desk or in the field!

Inside Microsoft Windows® SharePoint Services Version 3

Ted Pattison and Daniel Larson
ISBN 9780735623200

Get in-depth insights on Microsoft Windows SharePoint Services with this hands-on guide. You get a bottom-up view of the platform architecture, code samples, and task-oriented guidance for developing custom applications with Microsoft Visual Studio® 2005 and Collaborative Application Markup Language (CAML).

Inside Microsoft Office SharePoint Server 2007

Patrick Tisseghem
ISBN 9780735623682

Dig deep—and master the intricacies of Office SharePoint Server 2007. A bottom-up view of the platform architecture shows you how to manage and customize key components and how to integrate with Office programs—helping you create custom enterprise content management solutions.

Microsoft Office Communications Server 2007 Resource Kit

Microsoft Office Communications Server Team
ISBN 9780735624061

Your definitive reference to Office Communications Server 2007—direct from the experts who know the technology best. This comprehensive guide offers in-depth technical information and best practices for planning, designing, deploying, managing, and optimizing your systems. Includes a toolkit of valuable resources on CD.

Programming Applications for Microsoft Office Outlook® 2007

Randy Byrne and Ryan Gregg
ISBN 9780735622494

Microsoft Office Visio® 2007 Programming Step by Step

David A. Edson
ISBN 9780735623798

See more resources at **microsoft.com/mspress**
and **microsoft.com/learning**

Additional Resources for Business and Home Users

Published and Forthcoming Titles from Microsoft Press

Beyond Bullet Points: Using Microsoft® PowerPoint® to Create Presentations That Inform, Motivate, and Inspire
Cliff Atkinson • ISBN 0-7356-2052-0

Improve your presentations—and increase your impact—with 50 powerful, practical, and easy-to-apply techniques for Microsoft PowerPoint. With *Beyond Bullet Points*, you'll take your presentation skills to the next level—learning innovative ways to design and deliver your message. Organized into five sections, including Distill Your Ideas, Structure Your Story, Visualize Your Message, Create a Conversation, and Maintain Engagement—the book uses clear, concise language and just the right visuals to help you understand concepts and start getting better results.

Take Back Your Life! Special Edition: Using Microsoft Outlook® to Get Organized and Stay Organized
Sally McGhee • ISBN 0-7356-2215-9

Unrelenting e-mail. Conflicting commitments. Endless interruptions. In this book, productivity expert Sally McGhee shows you how to take control and reclaim something that you thought you'd lost forever—your work-life balance. Now you can benefit from Sally's popular and highly regarded corporate education programs, learning simple but powerful techniques for rebalancing your personal and professional commitments using the productivity features in Outlook. When you change your approach, you can change your results. So learn what thousands of Sally's clients worldwide have discovered about taking control of their everyday productivity—and start transforming your own life today!

On Time! On Track! On Target! Managing Your Projects Successfully with Microsoft Project
Bonnie Biafore • ISBN 0-7356-2256-6

This book focuses on the core skills you need to successfully manage any project, giving you a practical education in project management and how-to instruction for using Microsoft Office Project Professional 2003 and other Microsoft Office Professional Edition 2003 programs, such as Excel® 2003, Outlook 2003, and Word 2003. Learn the essentials of project management, including creating successful project plans, tracking and evaluating performance, and controlling project costs. Whether you're a beginner just learning how to manage projects or a project manager already working on a project, this book has something for you. Includes a companion CD with sample Project templates.

Design to Sell: Using Microsoft Publisher to Inform, Motivate, and Persuade
Roger C. Parker • ISBN 0-7356-2260-4

Design to Sell relates the basics of effective message creation and formatting to the specific capabilities built into Microsoft Publisher—the powerful page layout program found on hundreds of thousands of computers around the world. Many Microsoft Office users already have Publisher on their computers but don't use it because they don't think of themselves as writers or designers. Here is a one-stop guide to marketing that even those without big budgets or previous design or writing experience can use to create compelling, easy-to-read marketing materials. Each chapter has an interactive exercise as well as questions with answers on the author's Web site. Also on the Web site are downloadable worksheets and templates, book updates, more illustrations of the projects in the book, and additional before-and-after project makeovers.

Microsoft Windows® XP Networking and Security Inside Out: Also Covers Windows 2000
Ed Bott and Carl Siechert • ISBN 0-7356-2042-3

Configure and manage your PC network—and help combat privacy and security threats—from the inside out! Written by the authors of the immensely popular *Microsoft Windows XP Inside Out*, this book packs hundreds of timesaving solutions, troubleshooting tips, and work-arounds for networking and security topics—all in concise, fast-answer format.

Dig into the tools and techniques for configuring workgroup, domain, Internet, and remote networking, and all the network components and features in between. Get the answers you need to use Windows XP Service Pack 2 and other tools, tactics, and features to help defend your personal computer and network against spyware, pop-up ads, viruses, hackers, spam, denial-of-service attacks, and other threats. Learn how to help secure your Virtual Private Networks (VPNs), remote access, and wireless networking services, and take ultimate control with advanced solutions such as file encryption, port blocking, IPSec, group policies, and tamper-proofing tactics for the registry. Get up to date on hot topics such as peer-to-peer networks, public wireless access points, smart cards, handheld computers, wireless LANs, and more. Plus, the CD includes bonus resources that make it easy for you to share your new security and networking expertise with your colleagues, friends, and family.

For more information about Microsoft Press® books and other learning products, visit: **www.microsoft.com/mspress** *and* **www.microsoft.com/learning**

What do you think of this book?

We want to hear from you!

Do you have a few minutes to participate in a brief online survey?

Microsoft is interested in hearing your feedback so we can continually improve our books and learning resources for you.

To participate in our survey, please visit:

www.microsoft.com/learning/booksurvey/

...and enter this book's ISBN-10 number (appears above barcode on back cover*).
As a thank-you to survey participants in the United States and Canada, each month we'll randomly select five respondents to win one of five $100 gift certificates from a leading online merchant. At the conclusion of the survey, you can enter the drawing by providing your e-mail address, which will be used for prize notification only.

Thanks in advance for your input. Your opinion counts!

* Where to find the ISBN-10 on back cover

Example only. Each book has unique ISBN.